GOLD by
Moonlight
Lessons for Walking through Pain

I have a Savior; though I sought
    Through earth and air and sea
I could not find a word, a thought,
    To show Him worthily.
But planted here in rock and moss
I see the sign of utmost loss,
I hear a word—*On Calvary's cross,*
    Love gave Himself for thee.

GOLD by

Moonlight

Lessons for Walking through Pain

Amy Carmichael

PUBLICATIONS

Fort Washington, PA 19034

Gold by Moonlight
Published by CLC Publications

U.S.A.
P.O. Box 1449, Fort Washington, PA 19034

GREAT BRITAIN
51 The Dean, Alresford, Hants. SO24 9BJ

Copyright © 1935
The Dohnavur Fellowship

Reprinted by permission of
The Dohnavur Fellowship, England

This printing 2013

Printed in the United States of America

ISBN-10 (trade paper): 0-87508-087-1
ISBN-13 (trade paper): 978-0-87508-087-1
ISBN-13 (e-book): 978-1-61958-091-6

IN 1637, out of much trouble of mind, the Scottish minister Rutherford wrote to a friend: *It is possible to gather gold, where it may be had, with moonlight.*

This book is written to any who are walking in difficult places and who care to gather that gold.

Contents

Foreword

WHEN one's thoughts are running on any special line—I expect we have all noticed this—many little rays fall upon it. I had been thinking of "figures of the true," those lovely shadows of heavenly things which are everywhere about us, when I came upon this sentence in Amiel's *Journal Intime: "Everything is growing transparent to me. I see the types, the foundation of beings, the sense of things"*

Just then some photographs of the Austrian Tyrol and the Bavarian Highlands were given to me. These, as I looked at them, fell into a kind of order, and became for me figures of the true, transparent, full of the sense of things. Then came the thought of others, and so this book.

"And therefore if any word be therein that stirreth thee or comforteth thee more to the love of God, thank God, for it is His gift and not of the word. And if it comfort thee not, or else thou take it not readily, study not too long thereabout, but lay it beside thee till another time, and give thee to prayer or to another occupation. Take it as it will come, and not all at once."

A. C.
Dohnavur Fellowship
Tirunelveli District, South India

List of Illustrations

The photographs: They were given with such courtesy and kindness by Herr Groh of Munich, Herr Gaberell of Thalwil, and Dr. Defner of Innsbruck, that the pleasure of using them was doubled.

1

The Sense of Things

I SEE in this valley and mountain a general view of our years. We stand, when we are young, on the sunny slope among the pines, and look across an unknown country to the mountains. There are clouds, but they are edged with light. We do not fear as we dip into the valley; we do not fear the clouds. Thank God for the splendid fearlessness of youth. And as for older travelers whom Love has led over hill and dale, they have not been given the spirit of fear. They think of the way they have come since they stood on that bright hillside, and their word is always this: There are reasons and reasons for hope and for happiness, and never one for fear.

The mist and the clouds, and the light in the clouds, work together like separate notes in a tune; even the shadows of the pine trees on the grass have their part to play in making the picture. There is nothing that could be left out without loss. And it is so with the picture of our lives. We are called to believe this and to act as though we believed. (We were never meant to be like the host of the Egyptians when their chariot wheels fell off so that they drove them heavily.) We have the presence and the promises of God. We are meant to march to that great music.

Wrapped in the clouds and hidden by the mist is all that makes up life, its woods and ravines, its upland meadows where we go with much contentment, its hills called Difficulty, and its Delectable Mountains: in brief, its greater and smaller joys and sorrows, its trials of faith, disciplines, batterings of soul and body; all that our Saviour, in His story of the two builders, calls rain and floods and wind and the vehement beating of a stream.

There is no house of life out of reach of the stream. So, to be surprised when the rain descends and the floods come, and the winds blow and beat upon the house, as though some strange thing happened unto us, is unreasonable and unjust; it so miscalls our good Master, who never told us to build for fair weather or even to be careful to build out of reach of floods. "We must through much tribulation enter into the kingdom of God" is not a fair-weather word. "My son, if thou comest to serve the Lord, prepare thy soul for temptation." "Ye will not get leave to steal quietly to heaven, in Christ's company, without a conflict and a cross."

Even so, even though we must walk in the land of fear, there is no need to fear. The power of His resurrection comes before the fellowship of His sufferings.

2

The Dark Wood—Illuminated

WE need the Wine that maketh glad the heart of man and the Bread which strengtheneth man's heart as we begin our journey. The way is as various as this world of ours, this outer world that is "the pictured scroll of worlds within the soul," and sooner than we expected to see it, a dark wood crosses our path, and seems to forbid us to go on. And sometimes we forget immediately to look up to the light that pours into the wood from high above the trees, making it far more radiant than it is dark.

The clouding of the inward man which often follows accident, or illness, may be like a very dark wood. It can be strangely dulling and subduing to wake up to another day that must be spent between walls and under a roof; and a body that is cumbered by little pains—pains too small to presume to knock at the door of heaven, but not too small to wish they might—can sadly cramp the soul, unless it finds a way entirely to forget itself. Or the trouble may be the loss of means; poverty can be a darkness. The heavy overshadowing of bereavement is a very dark wood. ("Always wishing to consult one who is not here, groping by myself, with a constant sense of desolation," as Queen Victoria in the days of her early widowhood said piteously to Dean Stanley, whom she could trust to understand.) At such a time the miles that lie before us may appear one long night, without the companionship which made the twelve months of the year like the twelve gates of the City, each several month a pearl.

The partings of the nursery—we have all known them:

> Here a pretty baby lies
> Sung asleep with lullabies:
> Pray he silent and not stir
> Th' easy earth that covers her.

The old words are new somewhere every day. And there are those partings like that of the poet and his "Dear Son Gervase, whose winning love to me was like a friendship, far above the course of nature or his tender years." (For Gervase was only seven.) Father and little son have been together for three hundred years, and the pain of parting has long ago been blotted out; but in many a home there is a raw, red wound, and the healing of that wound seems very far away.

There are darker woods than illness, poverty, bereavement. There is the gloom wrapped about every thought of some catastrophe that has shaken the fabric of life to its foundations. There has not yet been full recovery from that shock. Broken hearts are everywhere in this world of tragedies: "How many there are, like the king in Samaria, wearing hidden sackcloth. Outside, the gay purple robe which, rent, reveals the secret. The people looked, and, behold, he had sackcloth within upon his flesh."

2

Just after Amiel, of whom it was said that he came to his desk as to an altar, received at the hands of his doctors the medical verdict which was his *arrêt de mort*, he wrote in his *Journal Intime*, "On waking it seemed to me that I was staring into the future with wide startled eyes. Is it indeed to *me* that these things apply? Incessant and growing humiliation, my slavery becoming heavier, my circle of action steadily narrower. What is hateful in my situation is that deliverance can never be hoped for, and that one misery will succeed another in such a way as to leave me no breathing space, not even in the future, not even in hope. All possibilities are closed to me, one by one." And he felt it difficult for the natural man to escape from a dumb rage against all this. (It is indeed not only difficult, it is impossible.) But he found the way of victory over the natural: "One word is worth all others, Thy will, not mine, be done," and he wrote at last *To will what God wills brings peace.*

But are such things as these which Amiel describes the will of God at all? The honest heart cannot be content with platitudes. "An enemy hath done this" is a word that reaches far and touches more than tares. If an enemy has done it, how can it be called the will of God?

3

We do not know the answer to that question now. But we have sidelights upon it, such as the vision in Revelation: They overcame him by the Blood of the Lamb and by the word of their testimony (victory through apparent defeat). And that other which shows the beast ascending out of the bottomless pit, and making war, and being victorious—but only for a little while. And as we rest our hearts upon what we know (the certainty of the ultimate triumph of good), leaving what we do not know to the Love that has led us all our life long, the peace of God enters into us and abides.

And then we see our light. And in that light we shall see light. We shall see Him who is the Light of the world, and so of all the woods in the world.

The entrance to the wood is dark. But we quickly pass through into light. The long, pure rays of that conquering light are interwoven with the tall stems of the trees, even as warp and woof, threads bright and dark, are interwoven in the web of our lives. But it is the bright threads that we shall see most clearly when we look upon the finished web. We are called to light, not to darkness.

So the forest in sunrise is a figure of the true. There is always light above us. Our roof is like the roof of the forest, transparent. So, verily, there is no roof; we live under open heavens. Look above the treetops, O my soul; from thence flow the fountains of light. See how that blessed light streams through the wood. See how it fills and floods and overflows the air with its splendor. Hear the word of the Lord thy Light: "Who is among you that feareth the Lord, that walketh in darkness and hath no light? Let him trust in the name of the Lord and stay himself upon his God." We have far too poor a conception of the intimacy with our God which He desires should be habitual. We are satisfied with too little and so we know too little of the light in the woods of life—that light which is always there.

<h1 style="text-align:center">4</h1>

For He is with us "all the days and all day long." The words come from something Bishop Moule said to the boys of Sherborne School: "A point of grammar can carry to us sometimes the very message of the Spirit. A tense, a case, a preposition, just because they are, in their measure, registers of the lightning-play of thought, may make all the difference to the force and fullness of a Scripture sentence. I do not think that I refine too much when I say that the original of 'all the days,' by the extending power of the accusatives, may justify the paraphrase, 'I am with you all the days, and all day long.'"

There was a traveler who at first saw nothing of the light that was shining in the wood. After a while the thought moved softly—*"I am with you all the days, and all day long."*

But just as a flower never presses its sweetness upon anyone but freely gives to him who desires it, and to him as often as he will, so that thought of peace did not force itself upon the traveler, and yet it did lovingly offer to his lips a cup of healing.

And then—but how it came to be so has never yet been told—the gloom of the darkness was gone, the light in the wood shone forth and the glory thereof.

3

The Ravine

1

THERE are level places high up in the forests which wrap our Indian mountains in evergreen, places where dawn is all green and gold, and any little stream that may be running there is first gold then silver. But he who would reach the higher peaks which lie open to the sun must descend steep slopes and thread shadowy ravines. The dull grass of this photograph, so different from the sunlit tussocks of the earlier picture, the forbidding gloominess of the trees and the ravine, convey that feeling of depression that the ill know so well, and the tired and the very anxious. More courage is required for a walk downhill into shadow than for the plunge into the dark wood which, after all, was splendidly lighted.

That weary way is a place of memories. One of the readings of Psalm 42 sees the soul sharpening the knives of pain by remembering jubilant yesterdays. "These things will I remember, how I passed on in the procession, how I marched with them to the house of God with the voice of joy and praise—a festive crowd." Yes, we were one of a festive crowd; was there any happy thing that we did not do? And we think of what used to be, so different from all that is now: "When I remember these things I pour out my soul in me." Was there ever a sad heart that did not feel like that?

And yet we are ashamed of such feelings, and the stronger part of us tries to encourage the weaker. "Why art thou cast down, O my soul? and why art thou disquieted in me? ["Why droopest thou, O my soul, and frettest so upon me?" is another reading.] Hope thou in God, for I shall yet praise Him for the help of His countenance." But soon the sadness has its way again—"O my God, my soul is cast down within me, my soul droops upon me."

Blessed be the tender mercy that has given us the truthful story of such hours, and with that story the prayer of release: "O send out Thy light and Thy truth: let them lead me; let them bring me unto Thy holy hill, and to Thy tabernacles." The mountain we are going to climb, the holy hill where His tabernacles are, is not in darkness. A broad beam of light falls upon that hill, a lighted path that leads to light like the pavement of heaven for clearness.

It is all true. We know that it is true. And yet there is something in the trend of our thoughts that is like the backwash of the waves, as wave after wave breaks on the shore. We have looked up. We have seen the lovely radiance of that upper air. But our feet must walk the ways of earth down that dreary hill, past those somber trees, and into the valley, before we can press up through the mist and stand under shining skies.

There is nothing imaginary about the oppression of the enemy, but there is deliverance from that oppression: "O my God, my soul is cast down within me: therefore will I remember Thee from the land of Jordan, and of the Hermanites, from the hill of Mizar."

2

I will remember Thee from the place where I am. Perhaps that place is a quiet room near another room where the surgeons are busy about their work. You have things to do, furniture to

arrange, a bed to prepare for the one who will soon be carried
in, but though you try to be absorbed in these matters you are
far more in that other room, all but seeing what is going on
there, all but hearing the quick words asking for this or that, and
the clink of the instruments. How loudly the clock ticks, how
slowly the minutes crawl. "He shall not be afraid of evil tidings;
his heart is fixed, trusting in the Lord": though evil tidings
come, the fixed and trusting heart shall not be afraid. But you
are afraid; so, is it that you do not trust? is your heart not fixed?
Do not stay to answer; there is a quicker way of help than that:
"O my God, my soul is cast down within me: *therefore will I
remember Thee.*" Here where deep calleth unto deep, and the
noise of the waterspouts, those cataracts of trouble, deafens me,
here just where I am, from the land of fear, the land of suspense,
will I remember Thee. And instantly the Lord commands His
lovingkindness.

Or your land of fear is different. It is the land where such
words as these are vital: *In God have I put my trust; I will not be
afraid; what can man do unto me?* and yet you are afraid. And
the minutes that crept so slowly outside the operation-room are
like running feet now. They are hurrying you to that same room.
What can man do unto you? Much every way. Like a small thing
unsheltered, like mimosa in a thunderstorm—stems, leaves,
flowers, involved in a common distress—that is how you feel till
you remember your God.

And then what happens? Who can tell? Who ever saw the
passing of the spirit of heaviness? the putting on of the garment
of praise? Only you *know* that the one has passed, and the other
has been put on. And you prove that the spirit of man energized
by the Spirit of God can defy the natural, and need not be, as it
would naturally be, destroyed when it is cast down. Its word is
always, Cast down but *not* destroyed: I will not fear what flesh
can do unto me—even my own flesh. For no Christian man or

woman was ever meant to walk on the natural plane. There is no provision made for such a walk. Always the expectation of God is that His child shall break through and live and endure as seeing the Invisible, and there is full provision made for him to do this: "My grace is sufficient for thee."

And now you are compassed about with songs. As one in a garden or in the greenwood at sunrise hears on all sides little snatches of song, a cadence or two, and sometimes long-sustained music of lovely liquid notes, so it is with you. Scriptures of comfort sing all around you now, and without effort on your part, words that make music are poured upon the inward ear.

> And when the strife is fierce, the warfare long,
> Steals on the ear the distant triumph song,
> And hearts are brave again, and arms are strong.
> > Alleluia.

But that is another kind of music. The singers are as little seen as the birds among the green leaves of the trees. And yet, like the birds, they are our dear companions. They are the heavenly people of the cloud of witnesses who compass us about.

For so the Lord commandeth His lovingkindness. Beneath, above, behind, before, that lovingkindness flows like broad rivers and streams. Where is fear then? Where is distress? The glorious Lord is unto us a place of broad rivers and streams wherein shall go no galley with oars, neither shall gallant ship pass thereby. The ships of the enemy cannot sail those waters. It is a thing forbidden. Fear thou not therefore, thou who art facing some inescapable trial of the flesh. *The Lord thy God will bear thee as a nursling.*[1] The Lord is thy shepherd, thou shalt not want. He shall gather the lambs with His arms and carry them in His bosom. We are all His lambs when we are ill.

The days or hours before the postman comes when a painful letter is expected, the moment between receiving a telegram and tearing it open, who does not know that land? It is a burning land. *Therefore will I remember Thee*—and the glowing sand becomes a pool, and we are quiet from fear of evil. There is also a sad-colored land which is not so full of fiery pangs as of one long ache. There is no suspense now. All is known. There is only a dull walk through a depressing valley and up into a mist. *Therefore will I remember Thee*, and Light and Truth are sent forth as guides, and Goodness and Mercy follow.

"It is a very dark valley," said a girl as she looked at the photograph. Only the evening before she had heard that her feet must walk down those slopes and into the valley. An hour afterwards she was heard singing to herself:

> Far hast Thou passed my prayer,
>   Good hast Thou been to me;
> Thy lover everywhere,
>   Blessed Will, cause me to be.

And we who loved her knew that she had looked beyond the valley to the light upon the hills. And we knew that even the valley would be light about her.

3

This book may find one who must thread the ravine at its darkest. There are wrongs done to innocence that scorch the mind. The indignation of the Lord waits upon the wrongdoer. It is a fearful thing to fall into the hands of the living God. If our Scripture showed no righteous Judge who has eyes like unto a flame of fire, the revelation of Love incarnate would be a shimmering dream. But this does not help the tortured in the hour of torture: "All Thy waves and Thy billows are gone over me. As with a sword in my bones mine enemies reproach me, while they say daily unto me, Where is thy God?"

And yet there is a lifting up: "Thou, which hast showed me great and sore troubles, shalt quicken me again, and shalt bring me up again from the depths of the earth."

"O thou afflicted, tossed with tempest, and not comforted, behold, I will lay thy stones with fair colors, and lay thy foundations with sapphires. And I will make thy windows of agates, and thy gates of carbuncles, and all thy borders of pleasant stones." Thou shalt be called "My delight is in her": thou shalt be called "My Pleasure."

Do not push the words away as too beautiful for you, you who have been trusted so. "Tell John what things ye have seen and heard; how that the blind see, the lame walk, the lepers are cleansed, the deaf hear, the dead are raised"—but though the Lord omnipotent walks so near thy prison, thou shalt be left in prison— "and blessed is he, whosoever shall not be offended in Me." That is the word for you. The Father trusts His broken child to trust: "If thou sink to dishonor, soar thou to love the honor of thy Beloved, who is sufficient to honor all that love Him. If thou be deceived and betrayed, rise thou in love even to the faithfulness of thy Beloved, by whom thou shalt be neither deceived nor betrayed. If thou sink through fear, soar thou through love till thou be safe with thy Beloved."[2]

It is to the trustful lover the Beloved says, "Fret not thyself because of the man who bringeth wicked devices to pass." Such words breathe so pure an air that only the faith that is born of love can live there. This that has come to pass could not have been had it not been allowed. Then Love allowed it. But why? We do not know. We cannot understand. "Wherein lies thy faith, O lover?" "My faith lies in this, that I believe things to be true that I understand not concerning my Beloved."

There is blessing prepared for the unoffended, and light no clouds of earth can smother, beyond the mist of the ravine. And in the end they shall walk up that pathway of light with their Beloved. "They shall walk with Me in white, for they are worthy."

4

But sometimes the place where we feel a desperate need to call upon our God, if we are to go on at all, may be quite ordinary, little, and in the eyes of others easy, not like the land of Jordan. ("How wilt thou do in the swelling of Jordan?" It is not like that.) Or the Hermons, those massive mountains from whose roots the Jordan sprang. ("Look from Hermon, from the lions' dens, from the mountains of the leopards." It is not like that.) So, as though to reassure the least of us in the least of small places, the Divine Author caused the writer of the psalm to choose a word which finds us where we are and says to us, "Fear not." For the hill Mizar is the Little Mountain. The word "Mizar" means *littleness*. It is the word used by Lot of Zoar: "Is it not a little one?" I will remember Thee from *the little hill*. [3]

Thrice blessed be the love that counts no place too little to be the place whence a cry can reach high heaven. O my Lord, I am but a little child; I know not how to go out or come in. No other would be overborne by so small a trial, neither would any other say of so short a travel, the journey is too great for me. O my God, I am ashamed and blush to lift up my face to Thee, but Thou, Lord, knowest Thy servant. Thou hast known my soul in adversities. Therefore from the hill Mizar, *the little hill*, will I remember Thee.

And *He* remembers *us*: many have told of a meeting on the road between the lover in his weakness, and Love, forever traveling in the greatness of His strength.

I used to wonder at the power of endurance I saw in the ill and the maimed. The mere thought of indoor life was anathema to me. How did they endure it? "The soul of the people was much discouraged because of the way"; were they never much discouraged? Did they never say, My soul cleaveth unto the dust: my soul melteth for heaviness? Did they never feel all but drowned in deep pools of utter weariness? I know the answer to those questions now. I know that the blast of the terrible ones can be like a storm against the wall. But I know what all who know Him whom they have believed would say if a younger child asked for the story of their years. It would be a simple story. It would not tell of untempted days but of succor that never failed:

> Love, traveling in the greatness of His strength,
>> Found me alone,
> Footsore and tired by the journey's length,
>> Though I had known,
> All the long way, many a kindly air,
> And flowers had blossomed for me everywhere.
>
> And yet Love found me fearful, and He stayed;
>> Love stayed by me.
> "Let not thy heart be troubled or dismayed,
>> My child," said He.
> Slipped from me then all troubles, all alarms;
> For Love had gathered me into His arms.

4

Snow

1

AND then suddenly—snow. And all our pleasant things are laid waste, or so indeed it seems, for we cannot see them anywhere; and all our newborn hopes are deep under the snow. For hopes had begun to be: a hope of healing, perhaps, if the trial be of the flesh; of a reversal of decision if it be something that lies in the power of another; or some touch on the wheel that turns our earthly affairs, if it concerns our circumstances; of some break somewhere, some natural human joy, some relief, some comfort in the aching sense of loss—and now the snow has fallen and covered everything.

In this cold picture a young fir has shaken off his load of snow; but our hopes were not hardy things like firs, they were made of more perishable stuff. We see ne sign of them. They are all under the blanket of snow, and there is an insidious push towards "the wasteful luxury of depression," or some other deadly form of spiritual indifference. What can we do? If the snow be not something against which we are meant to engage in spiritual warfare, a manifestation of the power of the prince of darkness whom we must always resist, then I know of only one answer: *In acceptance lieth peace.*

Things may be so that it is not easy to know whether we should resist or accept. And yet, if we wait a little, clearness will be given. Something will tell us. (Rather, Someone will tell us. The sheep know the Shepherd's voice.) Perhaps a verse of Scripture will be brought to mind and illuminated like a mountain peak in sunrise.

St. Paul dropped a shining thread that will lead us through the maze. He resisted injustice: Stripes—"Is it lawful for you to scourge a man that is a Roman?" Imprisonment—"I appeal unto Caesar."

But when stripes and imprisonment had to be endured, there is acceptance. He does not think of himself as Caesar's prisoner: "Paul, a prisoner of Jesus Christ." The steel chains of Caesar are his Lord's chains of gold. He is expecting deliverance ("I trust that through your prayers I shall be given unto you"), but we do not ever find him wrestling for his liberty with the rulers of the darkness of this world, who were behind the powers that had imprisoned him. His wrestling, laboring, agonizing, in prayer, was for others, not for himself. And even though he did not see the answer to all those prayers, he was so peacefully minded that he could lead others into peace.

2

Time as it passes makes a clear glass. We look through it and see things less as they appear when one is in the midst of them, more as God sees them from His eternity, where past, present, future are words unknown. Less than three hundred years can make such a glass. Take the six years between 1644 and 1650 in Scotland. Look at the struggle there, and the bitter suffering. See on one side the soldier, Montrose; on the other the minister, Rutherford.

They never met, never even dreamed that they were one in spirit, for they were in opposite camps, and victory to the soldier inevitably meant heartbreak to the minister. But hear Montrose, betrayed to a death of shame as men miscall such death: "I thank Him I go to heaven with joy the way He paved for me." Hear the other, when he rises to the higher air where his fellows cannot follow: "A cross of our own choosing, honeyed and sugared with consolations, we cannot have. I think not much of a cross when all the children of the house weep with me and for me; and to suffer when we enjoy the communion of the saints is not much; but it is hard when saints rejoice in the suffering of saints, and redeemed ones hurt (yea, even go nigh to hate) redeemed ones."

There speaks the man who suffered, just as the other suffered, for something greater than King or country, church or kirk. They met, though they did not know it, in that upper air. And now they are together where all differences of view are forgotten, and the things they fought for are forgotten too. And nothing of those six years seems worth remembering in comparison with that which was noble in the men who fought and struggled and trusted and were betrayed. Not the clash of swords, still less what made them clash, but the temper of those swords matters to us now. For the eternal stuff of history and of life is never found in the thunderclouds of dark enfolding circumstances, but always in the light that pierces the clouds. It is never the material, but always the spiritual that is deathless, and abides.

And so we come back to the thought which underlies this chapter. There is no strength to resist the ravaging lion as he prowls about seeking whom he may devour, unless our hearts have learned to accept the unexplained in our own lives, and the delays and disappointments and reverses which often come where our prayer for others seems to fall into silence and we see not our signs, and all is under snow.

3

Accept the snowfall as the appointed providence for the winter months, and wait till the voice which the winds obey calls to His south wind, "Blow upon My garden." (In the high Alps they watch for the *Föhn*; when it blows, the snow melts, and the upland meadows are like the valley of ripe corn in the psalm: they shout for joy, they also sing—they sing in flowers.)

To accept the will of God never leads to the miserable feeling that it is useless to strive any more. God does not ask for the dull, weak, sleepy acquiescence of indolence. He asks for something vivid and strong. He asks us to cooperate with Him, actively willing what He wills, our only aim His glory. To accept in this sense is to come with all the desire of the mind unto the place which the Lord shall choose, and to minister in the name of the Lord our God *there*—not otherwise. *Where the things of God are concerned, acceptance always means the happy choice of mind and heart of that which He appoints, because (for the present) it is His good and acceptable and perfect will.*

Dr. Way understands St. Paul's great Song of Contentment to mean this:

"He answered me, 'Sufficient for thee is My grace; it is in the forge of infirmity that strength is wrought to perfection.' Most cheerfully, then, will I boast of my frailty, rather than murmur, so that over me, as a tent, may be spread the might of Messiah. And so I am contented in the midst of frailty, outrages, sore straits, persecutions, privations, all for Messiah's sake; for it is just when I am frail that I am truly strong." The words *"in the midst of"* bring the thought down from cloudland to plain earth. And if it seems impossible to live so, "Rest upon God to do for you more than you can understand."

There is nothing cloudy or nebulous about a life lived on these peaceful lines. If the trial be illness, there is the prayer of faith, the obedience of faith, and a steadfast working together with the powers of healing. If it be the long strain of uncertainty, that weariest of all straining things, there is an eager and attentive and yet peaceful waiting, like the waiting of the little ship near the shore that was ready at the slightest sign to set sail with the Master; ready, too, to wait there till He made that sign. If the sorrow be an absence that must continue for a while, there is the refusal of disheartening, weakening thoughts and the settling of the will to lay hold upon words of everlasting consolation. Unreserved acceptance opens the way for the turning of the captivity—"whoso offereth thanksgiving glorifieth Me and prepareth a way that I may show him the salvation of God." It makes for the quickening of life under the snow, and for the serenity which flows from interior peace.

> O thou beloved child of My desire,
> Whether I lead thee through green valleys,
>> By still waters,
>> Or through fire,
> Or lay thee down in silence under snow,
> Through any weather, and whatever
>> Cloud may gather,
>> Wind may blow—
> Wilt love Me? trust Me? praise Me?

Then there is what the Septuagint calls a "Song of Pause." This is the snow song of a contented heart, answering the question of its Lord, "Wilt love Me? trust Me? praise Me?" It comes before the shouting song of the flowers and the yellow corn.

The snow-time is full of quiet secrets too, for we are carefully keeping secrets with our God about the growing things under the snow, secrets like those a child keeps with its mother, little private understandings not to be spoken aloud. A glance, a smile, a touch of the hand—that is their speech.

Sometimes there are beautiful things that would not have been if there had not been snow. "There were never any prisons of suffering that I was in, but still it was for the bringing multitudes more out of prison," said George Fox after his bitterest snowstorm. These inward cherishings of joy lead to what the older Friends called "a cool and tender Frame of spirit." There is no futile restlessness: if we have hope that another may be helped by something we have found under the snow.

4

The psalms are full of Songs of Pause for times of snow. Such songs are not jocund. There is no dancing with the daffodils. That comes afterwards. But there is trust. The Songs of Pause are songs of trust. And as these Songs of Pause enter into the quieted soul and fill it with peace, the snow loses its power to chill and to crush.

There is peace in this picture of snow, and beneath it is the nurturing of life. And so at last we come to something exultant: O ye Frost and Cold, O ye Ice and Snow, bless ye the Lord, praise Him and magnify Him forever. And out of the silence of the snow we shall hear the voice of the words, but we shall see no similitude; only we shall hear a voice.

There are some for whom snow must mean such dense darkness that the mind cannot conceive of any light piercing through. As well hope to cage a rainbow and carry it down to them. Behold I am the Lord, the God of all flesh, is there anything too hard for Me? Ah, Lord God, behold, Thou hast made the heaven and the earth by Thy great power and stretched-out arm, and there is nothing too hard for Thee. I know that Thou canst do everything. And yet?

That unspoken question has racked many a heart, especially when some distress has made the thought of others in greater distress intolerable. We forget that something good may be happening for their help, something almost unbelievably good:

Through the dark and silent night
On Thy radiant smiles I dwelt;
And to see the dawning light
Was the keenest pain I felt.

That was written by Madame Guyon, who suffered in every sensitive fiber of her being. The words may seem too high for earth. But it is not for us to set a limit to what God is prepared to do when He is training a soul to endure, not accepting deliverance.

Still, these far-flying words were written three hundred years ago. Wonderful things happened then. A letter, slipped into a book by mistake less than twenty years ago, has lately reappeared as such things kindly do sometimes. It was written from Auckland Castle soon after Mrs. Moule's death had left the Bishop very lonely, for his daughter Tesie had died a little while before, and his only other child was married. He writes of comfort "dropped like an anodyne from the hand of the Physician into my great wound. (He gives no anesthetics, but He does give anodynes.) I bless Him who is more near and dear to me than ever, in His mercy. My beloved one is not far from me. And I bless her Lord for calling her to go upstairs, and meet Him there, and our Tesie with Him, and for trusting me to meet the solitude here, and to find Him very near in it."

So near is the eternal Comforter that the strangely un-Christian view of death of our half-pagan age does not come into the picture at all. The wife is not "lost." She is just "upstairs."

The same thought moves in an older letter written to a daughter about her mother. "She is now above the Winter with a little change of place, not of a Saviour; only she enjoyeth Him now without messages, and in His own immediate presence, from whom she heard by letters and messengers before." Her joy is like the joy "of finding the first summer rose."

Those who think like that know the way to the wells where Bunyan drank. They do not speak of the "alarming illness" of a fellow pilgrim. Such illness is "an arrow with a point sharpened with love let easily into the heart." "Lamented death" is a phrase they never use; and they no more dream of "going into mourning" when a friend puts on immortality than the flowers dream of darkening their fair colors when one of their number is gathered. (Black here, while There, "Lo, as they entered they were transfigured; and they had raiment put on that shone like gold!") If only we cared to drink of those wells, we should see more clearly, and perhaps almost hear the bells of the City ring to welcome the travelers thereto.

The letter from a lonely study in a lonely house with its gentle "no anesthetic but anodynes" will waken echoes in many a land. And those echoes will repeat the older word: "Because Thy lovingkindness is better than life, my lips shall praise Thee. Because Thou hast been my help, therefore in the shadow of Thy wings will I rejoice." What to our eyes is a very pit of darkness is to those children of His love only the shadow of His wings.

From the Further East a letter came to this house last mail. It was written in a prison house of pain, the kind by common consent most dreaded, but it does not make one think of a somber life under snow but of snow in sunshine, as our picture shows it, or even the sparkle where here and there the sunlight picks out a crystal. Enclosed in that letter is a quotation from a song written by a leper. His hands are gone and he writes with a pen tied on to the poor remnant of an arm: "To the heart aglow for Thee," he wrote, "the Valley of the Shadow is like sunrise on the sea." O Lord, Thou art wonderful. Thou canst make a radiance anywhere. There is *nothing* too hard for Thee.

5

The more we learn of the many-colored tissue of life the more we discover that our kind Lord has as many ways of meeting His children as there are trials to flesh and to spirit. Perhaps one of the weariest trials is the heavy feeling of uselessness to God and man that comes down like snow on the heart. Any deprivation would be welcome if only we had something to offer to our Lord or to the least of our fellow servants. And we think of the wise men from the East, who opened their treasures and presented unto Him gifts, gold and frankincense and myrrh. Happy wise men. All the toils of their travel must have been forgotten when they poured out their precious things before Him. Why have we nothing to offer when they had so much? We have nothing now but our poor love to give.

To a heart troubled by this question came one day a strange reply: "Thou gavest Me no water for My feet: thou gavest Me no kiss." For a moment that heart waited, not understanding; but presently, softly, these other words came: "To love that could miss so small a sign of love as water, and a kiss, is not love the dearest offering?"

> And may we all be Thine own Marys, Lord?
> Dear worthy Lord, how courteous Love's reward:
> For all the little that I give to Thee,
> Thou gavest first to me.

> Rich is Thy harvest, O Thou Corn of Wheat:
> A cloud of lovers gather round Thy feet.
> What miracle of love that Thou shouldst miss
> Low on Thy feet, one kiss.

But even as one writes one waits, while the candles of God do their work. *Whatsoever ye have spoken in darkness shall be heard in the light.* Those words are searching candles. What word was spoken in darkness under the snow? What word was spoken in the ear of God alone? Our Lord did not say, "Whatsoever ye have said aloud, whatsoever ye have written in a letter or a book," but "Whatsoever ye have spoken in darkness where no man was, that most private word 'in the ear'"—*that* word shall be heard in the light, that word shall be spoken on the housetops.

Try me, O God, and search the ground of my heart. Let there be spiritual honesty there. So cleanse, so keep, so fill that inner chamber, that when whatsoever was spoken in darkness shall be heard in the light, and when that which was spoken in Thine ear in closets shall be proclaimed upon the housetops, it may abide the judgment of the light.

5

After the Snow

1

"FOR, lo, the winter is past, the rain is over and gone; the flowers appear on the earth; the time of the singing of birds is come, and the voice of the turtledove is heard in our land." And the trees of the wood sing out at the presence of the Lord, till the world that was so cold and snowy is like the young daughter who dreamed of unhappiness and waked herself with laughing.

But that of which the ruin in the picture is the symbol was not a dream. Nor is it now as a dream when one awaketh. The trouble which grieved the night has not floated off on the wings of the morning. There has been a turning of the captivity and the hard weather has passed, but there is still something stark in our landscape, like the ruin in the midst of the white cherry. There is a fact, a memory, a possibility, that strikes up and faces us wherever we look. That knot of painful circumstances is there; that fear, that fearful thing, may be waiting in the shadows to spring upon us like a panther on a fawn. These things still are; it would be a kind of falsehood to act as though they were not.

The picture is a figure of the true: it is full of grace and a lovely lightness, but it is the ruin that arrests the eye and gives character to the whole. Take it out, and you have merely a pretty page of scenery, and life is more than that. The charm of leaf and bud after a time of snow is not all that God has for those whom He is preparing to minister to others.

2

"When heaven is about to confer a great office on a man it always first exercises his mind and soul with suffering, and his body to hunger, and exposes him to extreme poverty, and baffles all his undertakings. By these means it stimulates his mind, hardens his nature, and enables him to do acts otherwise not possible to him," wrote Mencius, the Chinese sage, two thousand years ago; and the illustration of the Chladni plate beautifully shows how these agitating circumstances can be caused to work together. You sprinkle sand on a brass plate fixed on a pedestal, and draw a bow across the edge of the plate, touching it at the same time with two fingers. Then, because of this touch, the sand does not fall into confusion but into an ordered pattern like music made visible. Each little grain of sand finds its place in that pattern. Not one grain is forgotten and left to drift about unregarded.

There is nothing in the vibrations of the bow to make a pattern. Suffering, hunger, poverty, baffling circumstances cannot of themselves make anything but confusion. But if there be the touch of the Hand, all these things work together for good, not for ill, not for discord, but for something like the harmony of music.

So the ruin is not out of sight, and thoughts wander round it at times: If it be loss, there is still an aching absence; if it be difficult circumstances, they still dominate the landscape; if it be limitations, they still confine us. "Let me exaggerate nothing," wrote Amiel as he contemplated his ruin, "my liberty is negative. Nobody has any hold over me, but many things have become impossible to me, and if I were so foolish as to wish for them, the limits of my liberty would soon become apparent. Therefore I take care not to wish for them, and not to let my thoughts dwell on them. I only desire what I am able for, and in this way I run my head against no wall. I cease even to be conscious of the boundaries which enclose me. I take care to wish for rather less than is in my power, that I may not even be reminded of the obstacles in my way. Renunciation is the safeguard of dignity. Let us strip ourselves, if we would not be stripped."

But to stop there is to lose all. What if the crash of hopes, the heartbreak, this that piles itself up as the ruin in the picture of life, does truly make more manifest what our Book calls the Beauty of the Lord? If that be so, we should not wait till we are where life's poor ruins will appear as the tumbled bricks of a child's castle before we let our hearts take comfort from such words as these: "I know the thoughts that I think toward you, saith the Lord, thoughts of peace and not of evil, to give you an expected end." Rotherham understands God's thoughts to mean His plans: *"I know the plans which I am planning for you, plans of welfare and not of calamity, to give you a future and a hope."* Thoughts of peace for our prayers, for our intercessions for others which seem to be ineffective ("When He had heard, He abode two days still in the same place where He was"); a future and a hope for the prayers that we feared were covered by the snow, and for those others that appeared to fall to earth like the falling stars that break and scatter into nothingness as we watch them—even those prayers are folded up in the thoughts of peace that He thinks toward us.

These words are for us. We may take them though they were spoken to another people in another age. All the green fields of the Scriptures are for all the sheep of His pasture; none are fenced off from us. Our Lord and Saviour, that great Shepherd of the sheep, Himself led the way into these fields, as a study of His use of the Old Testament shows. His servants, the writers of the New Testament, followed Him there; and so may we. The words of the Lord about His thoughts of peace are for us as well as for His ancient people Israel.

Hammer this truth out on the anvil of experience—this truth that the loving thoughts of God direct and perfect all that concerneth us; it will bear to be beaten out to the uttermost. The pledged word of God to man is no puffball to break at a touch and scatter into dust. It is iron. It is gold, that most malleable of all metals. It is more golden than gold. It abideth imperishable forever. If we wait till we have clear enough vision to see the expected end before we stay our mind upon Him who is our Strength, we shall miss an opportunity that will never come again: we shall never know the blessing of the unoffended. Now is the time to say, "My heart is fixed, O God, my heart is fixed: I will sing and give praise," even though as we say the words there is no sense of exultation. *"It is possible to gather gold, where it may be had, with moonlight,"* by which I understand something less helpful than daylight would be in the search and the finding of gold. By moonlight, then, let us gather our gold.

3

For Amiel there was no facile gathering of gold. (I quote him in different moods because he is so human and so honest, never posing, and incapable of cant. He is always earnestly exposing his inmost thoughts to the searchlight of truth.) When he knew the course that his disease was likely to take, he asked himself what he believed about the government of the world. Was it in the hands of "an indifferent Nature? A Satanic principle of things? A good and just God? Three points of view. The second is improbable and horrible. The first appeals to our stoicism. The third alone can give joy. Only, is it tenable? Is there a particular Providence directing all the circumstances of our life?" Finally he comes to this: there is such a God; it is possible to triumph over pain and death. In willing what God commands, in consenting to what He takes from us or refuses—in this we find our peace.

"What does the apotheosis of the cross mean, if not the death of death, the defeat of sin, the raising to the skies of voluntary sacrifice, the defiance of pain—O Death, where is thy sting? O Grave, where is thy victory? By long brooding over this theme—the agony of the just, peace in the midst of agony, and the heavenly beauty of such peace—humanity came to understand that a new religion was born, a new mode, that is to say, of explaining life and of understanding suffering."

Sometimes in an hour of deep fatigue his light burns dimly, but always spiritual airs fan the fainting flame, and it rises and triumphs. "What dupes we are of our own desires! Destiny has two ways of crushing us—by refusing our wishes and by fulfilling them. But he who only wills what God wills escapes both catastrophes. All things work together for his good." After seven years' illness and after the fourteenth night running in which he had been consumed by sleeplessness, he is still set on doing the last things well. Five days later he writes his last words, "My flesh and my heart fail me." *"Que vivre est difficile, o mon coeur fatigue!"* And then his Lord said, "It is enough"; and what Amiel's next words were we do not know.

Only we know he became at that moment a companion of immortals. He saw then as they see. He saw why suffering must be the law of life. He saw his ruin not like a black rock jutting harshly through the white spray of the flowers, but like unto a stone most precious, even like a jasper stone clear as crystal.

The ruin accepted as part of our landscape, the loss accepted for love of our dear Lord, bears the image of the earthy now; but the day will come when (like ourselves) it will bear the image of the heavenly. For, said our Lord and Saviour before He was offered up, "He that findeth his life shall lose it: and he that loseth his life for My sake shall find it."

Now in the place where He was crucified there was a garden, and ever since in every garden of His lovers there has been a cross.

6

Cherry Blossoms

THE sunshine is streaming into my little room; and I can see (by twisting my head) a tiny glimpse of the sky. It is a joy to feel the air coming on my face, though sometimes, and particularly in the spring, I have a big longing to get right out of doors beyond four walls, and to feel the wind and sunshine, and the rain too, upon me.

"It is twenty-one years this year since I could sit up, and for nineteen years it has been this one position in bed; but isn't it wonderful that He enables us to triumph, and to rejoice in Him?

"Some anemones traveled to me from Edinburgh the other day, and they look fresh and beautiful still. Then I have two little primroses, and a scrap of moss, and several daffodils from a garden in Ayrshire." This from a recent letter brought the cherry blossoms into this book.

The power to find pleasure not only in the masses of blossoms that gather round the ruin of human hope, but in each spray, and more—in the very petals and stamens of each little flower, and even in the faint pencil-line of the shadow of the stamen on the petal—is one of the dearest gifts that is given to the Lord's bondmen. It is common to them all.

"Old cast clouts and rotten rags"[4]—one would not naturally write such unpleasant words on the same page as "cherry blossoms." But the spirit that characterizes this happy letter is the same as that which caused the prisoner Jeremiah, who was drawn up from the miry dungeon in Jerusalem 2,500 years ago, to remember the rags that kept his "armholes" from being cut by the cords. There is always something to be happy about if we look for it:

> Two men looked through prison bars,
> The one saw mud, the other stars.

2

Can we ever thank Him enough for the spirit of happiness? "Not taking upon us, by feigning, more than we have in feeling"—but the spirit of happiness cannot be feigned. That spirit is genuine, or it is not there at all. There is something in the continuance of happiness in untoward circumstances that is like the power of rejuvenescence in the rotifer. This little creature, which we find sometimes by scores in a drop of water, is a thing so delicate that a slip of the cover glass on the slide will destroy the pinpoint of life in its crystal vase. And yet, when the pond dries up, it can gather itself into a ball within which are the forces of life. Then after being blown about by the wind perhaps for years, in a state of utter dustiness; when the rotifer finds itself in its own element the ball will revive, and put forth foot and head and silver wheel, and be as it was before, a minute marvel of activity and apparent enjoyment.

The spirit of happiness is sheer miracle. It is the gift of the happy God, as Paul names our heavenly Father in writing to Timothy. It is the gift of the God of love. He pours it out of His own fountains, through unseen channels, as He poured it upon Paul and Silas before their feet were taken out of the stocks and their stripes washed; for "no created powers in hell, or out of hell, can mar the music of our Lord Jesus, nor spoil our song of joy." But it often pleases Him to give it through the hands of His Ebed-melechs (Servant of the King, a good name for those who bring alleviations to suffering people). And when they bring sprays of cherry blossoms too, surprises of love, then Another comes into the room, and our heart runs out to meet Him.

> O Love Divine, if we can see
>> In our beloved so dear a grace,
> When Love unveils, what will it be
>> To see Thee face to face?

There are some for whom illness is made more difficult than it need be. Boswell shivers on the chilly boat journey from Greenwich to London, "for the night air was so cold that it made me shiver. I was the more sensible of it from having sat up all the night before, recollecting and writing in my journal what I thought worthy of preservation" (of the sayings and doings of his friend). But Johnson, who "was not in the least affected by the cold, scolded me as if my shivering had been a paltry effeminacy." Another unfortunate is rebuked for a headache: "At your age, Sir, I had no head-ach." There is one simple way to achieve serenity when (if ever) we meet Dr. Samuel Johnson: It is to be glad that he has never known "shivering" or "head-ach." And also to remember that he is probably like a Spanish chestnut, rather prickly outside, but inside very good.

One of the great secrets of happiness is to think of happy things. There were many unhappy things in Philippi, things false, dishonorable, unjust, impure, hideous and of very bad report; the air of Philippi was darkened by these things. The Christians of that town might easily have had their lives stained by continually letting their thoughts dwell on what they could not help seeing and hearing and feeling, the evil which they must often have met and fought in their striving together for the faith of the gospel. But they were definitely told to think of things true, honorable, just, pure, lovely and of good report. "And if there be any virtue, and if there be any praise, think on these things."

There is a temptation of thought which can torment the ill: the temptation to compare the past with the present. Stephen Phillips' *A Poet's Prayer* seizes this nettle, and it turns into an herb of healing in his hands:

> That I have felt the rushing wind of Thee;
> That I have run before Thy blast to sea;
> That my one moment of transcendent strife
> Is more than many years of listless life;
> Beautiful Power, I praise Thee.

And now that he is not "rapt in hurry to the stars," but instead of the great freedom of the skies must quietly front the life that lingers after zest, he turns to his God:

> 'Tis not in flesh so swiftly to descend,
> And sudden from the spheres with earth to blend;
> Sustain me in that hour with Thy left hand,
> And aid me, when I cease to soar, to stand;
> Make me Thy athlete even in my bed,
> Thy girded runner, though the course be sped.

What is my heart's desire? Relief from the fatigue of the race? the peace that is the dearth of pain? the cherry flowers of earth? Those blossoms may be given, but if not (and if so) there remains the prayer, *Make me Thy athlete even in my bed*.

And to His athlete the Lord presently gives something better than the crown of wild olive cut with the golden sickle. He gives His calm which "is that white where all the colors are." And then He gives the crown of Lombardy—the crown which has iron set under the gold. It is the iron that gives significance to that crown. Without the iron, which men thought of as beaten out of one of the nails that pierced our Saviour's flesh, it would have been as other crowns, a trivial matter of gold and gems. The iron does not show; it is not meant to show. The Iron Crown is a private matter between lover and Beloved.

The supreme thing is to wear that crown courageously; and thankfully too, for it is a wonderful thing to be asked to wear it. One of our Indian viceroys, perhaps the most dazzling figure of them all, could not stand to face an audience without the support of a steel device. "I, at times, suffer terribly from my back," he wrote from out of the blaze of public life, "and one day it will finish me. But so long as one is marching, I say, let the drums beat and the flags fly." (Not many knew of that gnawing pain. Perhaps if it were remembered that often there is sackcloth under royal robes, the judgment of the world would be kinder.)

Whatever the Iron Crown may be, so long as one is marching let the drums beat and the flags fly. What does it matter that no one knows the cost of those brave words? He whose crown was of thorn knows all that is covered from casual glance of man. Where others see merely a decorous exterior, He sees a soul, sometimes a tortured soul, looking up into His eyes for courage and grace to live triumphantly a moment at a time. And if we could hear spiritual voices speak, we should hear something like this: "Thy flesh and thy heart faileth? I know, My child, I know. But I am the strength of thy heart and thy portion forever. Thou shalt not be forgotten of Me."

7

Rough Water

1

THERE are no words of comfort like those that our Father speaks to us: *When thou passest through the waters, I will be with thee; and through the rivers, they shall not overflow thee.* We are called to go straight through the foaming river holding fast to this assurance.

And we look at the white water. There are potholes among the boulders where a foot might be caught and held; a sudden spate might easily overwhelm us; the spray half blind us; the noise deafen us. There is no human way, no human hope; there is nothing to be seen but a boiling flood, boulders, snags, tossing spray; there is not one inch of smooth water anywhere. But the word of our God holds fast. It would be cowardice to fear. God save us from cowardice. "Be of good cheer, my brother; I feel the bottom, and it is good."

But life can be terrific. Things can happen that seem to tear such words out of our mouth and drive them like dust before a hurricane. Look at that shattered life, that young life, and tell me of a God of mercy and pity—how can you?

Is to rack souls joy?
Does turn of screw make songs? or hammering
Of most unkindly fortune waken music?
Such hammers fall too heavily for that.

Those hammers fall on many hearts today; and only He whose prayer in Gethsemane began with the words, "O My Father, if it be possible, let this cup pass from Me," can enable the soul of man in its extremity to continue that prayer as He continued it, and to end it as He ended it. *There are times in life when the one Place in all the world where we can find what we are seeking is the Garden of Gethsemane.*

From that garden it is only a few steps to a place which is called in the Hebrew Golgotha, where they crucified Him. Our questions are hushed there.

"If thou be the Son of God, come down from the cross. . . . Let him save himself, if he be Christ, the Chosen of God. . . . If thou be Christ, save thyself and us. . . . Let be, let us see whether Elias will come to save him." *If? Whether?* And to all, silence in heaven above, in earth beneath. There was no vindication by God, no opening of the heavens, no Spirit of God descending like a dove and lighting upon the Holy One, no Voice declaring, "This is My beloved Son." And He, the blessed Sufferer, was silent—as a sheep before her shearers is dumb so He opened not His mouth to answer any question, till on an evening, as He walked along a country road with two troubled men, He said, *Ought not Christ to have suffered these things, and to enter into His glory?*

That silence shames us. Cannot we, His foolish ones and blind, bid our restless questions be still awhile? It is only for a little while, for it is toward evening now, and the day is far spent. Soon, very soon we shall go in to tarry with Him. All our questions will be answered then. But in that day we shall ask Him nothing: "Ye shall ask Me no question," so He has told us. Perhaps because we shall have forgotten our questions. One look in His face, and like the dew that has seen the sun those questions will have vanished. Vanished as a cloud in the blue that is as though it had never been.

2

Strange things can happen in the short day of life. I am allowed to copy a page from a letter written by one who nursed his fellow missionary through deadly illness, in the hope that should this page find another on the edge of that rough water he may feel the handgrasp of a friend.

"The book [*Rose From Brier*] found its way into the sickroom on the ground that it might have a message for the patient, but he soon passed beyond the reach of words of cheer. I have never before realized how satanic delirium can be. It seems as if the devil is allowed to take advantage of the weakened condition of the sufferer to dominate his mind. These nights I have seen a soul suffering the very agonies of hell, confirmed in the belief that he had fallen from grace and was doomed to everlasting damnation; and then the same child of God convinced that he was a devil, and acting like one. The mention of the Name would but call forth blasphemy. There is something sinister and devilish about these diseases. Thank God we do not need to understand."

There is no new thing under the sun:

"One thing I would not let slip," wrote John Bunyan. "I took notice that now poor Christian was confounded, that he did not know his own voice; and thus I perceived it: just when he was come over against the mouth of the burning pit, one of the wicked ones got behind him, and stepped up softly to him, and whisperingly suggested many grievous blasphemies to him, which he verily thought had proceeded from his own mind. This put Christian more to it than anything that he met with before, even to think that he should now blaspheme Him that he loved so much before: yet, if he could have helped it, he would not have done it; but he had not the discretion either to stop his ears, or to know from whence these blasphemies came.

"When Christian had traveled in this disconsolate condition some considerable time, he thought he heard the voice of a man as going on before him saying, 'Though I walk through the Valley of the Shadow of Death, I will fear no ill; for Thou art with me.'

"Then was he glad, and that for these reasons: *First*, because he gathered from thence that some who feared God were in this Valley as well as himself. *Secondly*, for that he perceived God was with them, though in that dark and dismal state. And why not, thought he, with me? though, by reason of the impediment that attends this place, I cannot perceive it. *Thirdly*, for that he hoped, could he overtake them, to have company by and by.

"So he went on, and called to him that was before: but he knew not what to answer for that he also thought himself alone. And by and by the day broke. Then said Christian, 'He hath turned the shadow of death into the morning.'"

Thank God for the morning after such a night. About the piteous fading of the mind, someone has said, "It is sometimes the Father's way to put His child to bed in the dark"; but the child will waken very happy in the morning. And the words comfort the greater trial of what appears to be spiritual collapse. However shadowed the "going to bed" of the Father's child may be, the awakening will be radiant.

Think of it and be comforted, you who have seen one dear to you pass unsuccored, apparently, through rough waters. Body, soul and spirit may appear to be submerged, but the spirit of the child of God is never for one moment imperiled, no sudden swirl shall pluck it out of the Hands that hold it fast. And your prayer found it where you could not follow. There was no response that you heard or saw when you spoke those words of life, and sang those hymns by that bedside. But singing can follow one under water; it sounds far off and a little dreamy, but it is clear. Perhaps that is how those hymns sounded to that dear spirit. And under water, deep under water, it saw a light softly diffused coming to meet it. This is what happens when one dives into a deep pool at night and swims slowly upward. The moonlight meets one long before one reaches the surface. And if it can be so with the moonlight of earth, how much more true it must be of the sunlight of heaven.

3

There are many rooms in the House of Pain. I have asked that I may not miss any room where a reader of this book is or shall be. A daughter writing of her beautiful mother shall speak for me:

"There were days—sad days they were—when her faith was tuned to the minor key; when the note it struck was one of wistful yearning, of a blind 'holding on' in the dark, not any longer of victorious progress from strength to strength. In the last sad year, when those who loved her longed and prayed for some very special vision of faith and conviction to support her—who all her life had staked everything on the venture of faith—it was not given."[5]

Behind that sentence lie such gallant years that I think the angels must have marveled. "That now unto the principalities and the powers in heavenly places might be made known through the church the manifold wisdom of God" ("the wisdom which is never at a loss to carry out its purposes of grace, be the problems presented by its subject what they may"), her life illustrated those words. And yet this last boon was withheld. "And I cannot help wondering why," said one in speaking of a similar denial; "I should have expected an entrance 'in full sail' for all such heroic souls."

Perhaps one of the pleasures of heaven will be found in the shining forth of the answer to such questions, if indeed they have not vanished like the dew and the cloud; but now we know in part, and the answer in part is this: There are some whom our Lord has so proved that He can trust them with any withholding, even the withholding of light. To one whose mind was as clear as her faith was true there could hardly have been a more searching test of endurance, nor could one more painful have been asked of those whom she loved. But their Lord could trust them too. And as the so great a cloud of witnesses compassed about the traveler, then. very nearly Home, what must have been their loving joy as they saw her cross that bar of shadow and walk into the Land of Light?

As I pondered the matter I remembered something I had not wished to be in the last word of this book. We had to search for the picture. Several were sent to us, but either the bright path ended in a dark sky or dark hills, or there was something else about it which made it not just what I wanted. (I wanted darkness, but not ultimate darkness; clouds, but light beyond; and on the water a clear path of unbroken light.) The only possible picture had a break on the lighted path. And I regretted this.

I see its purpose now. It is the perfect figure of the true, for, to some, that break in the brightness is the final trial of their faith. Beyond the narrow darkness is brightness that grows brighter and brighter, never to darken again. And beyond and above, never for one moment dimmed, the blessed light is shining. That bar of shadow will look very narrow when it has been crossed.

This thought of crossing a shadow to walk into light may help to comfort a distress about what ignorance calls an "untimely death" (as though anything untimely could possibly be in the life of one whose times are in the hand of God). It must have been delightful for Enoch when, as a child said, "He walked so far that he could not come back, but just went on." Sometimes it is different, and then the angels are sent to carry the one who is tired of walking. Do they say to him, "Let us go into the House of the Lord"? If they do, perhaps his heart replies in long-familiar words, "I was glad when they said unto me, Let us go into the House of the Lord." When that is so we almost hear another word: "If ye loved Me, ye would rejoice, because I said, I go unto the Father."

And if there was not that happy going, but only a disabling accident, then the call to you, his friend, is to conquering faith. Spiritual marvels are wrought in answer to the prayer of faith. In the days of the great struggle for the freedom of Italy the vile prisons of Naples and elsewhere were crowded with tortured men, heavily chained. And they were there for life. In the prison song of one, Giovanni Nicotera, there are haunting words about what God can do for captive men:

> "No darkness is so deep, but white
>   Wings of the angels through can pierce;
>   *Nor any chain such heaps lies in*
>   *But God's own hand can hold it light;*
>   Nor is there any flame so fierce
>   But Christ Himself can stand therein."

4

There is a pain that can gnaw like a wolf. Perhaps a word might have been spoken, or a letter written, that would have prevented a journey which ended disastrously, as we on earth use the word. But God has a thousand ways of turning His child back from the wrong path: He can make even asses talk, when those who could speak better are absent or silent. "I being in the way, the Lord led me" must be true, however things appear, and we torment our hearts in vain when we forget this.

What if He, for reasons not told yet, hindered the speaking of that preventing word, the writing of that letter? He can guide by withholding rays of light as well as by causing them to illuminate a path.

We are far too complex in our thoughts of the mercy of God. We need to be simple, and willing to accept simple comfort.

There is quietness and assurance forever in the simplicity of our Lord's words when "for the first time He opens heaven to faith" and speaks of the many mansions of His Father's House.[6] He is speaking of something better than mere dwelling places where adventure ends, and we settle down, as it were. The "mansions" are resting places like the stations on the great roads of olden times, where travelers found refreshment as they journeyed on—this was a new revelation about the heavenly life. And our Lord says of this surprising thing, "If it were not so, I would have told you."

Vistas open with the word. We have been about our Father's business on the dusty roads of earth. We shall soon be traveling on those other roads; on what errands we are not told, whence and whither we are not told. Do the stars light those great roads like mighty street lamps? We do not know. Only one thing we know: this immeasurable joy, these discoveries of joy will be ours. tomorrow—if it were not so our Lord Jesus would have told us.

We are always moving towards unimaginable happiness though as yet we see only a shadow of good things to come, not the very image of the things. But they are eternal in the heavens. The most satisfying answer to all the questions (that we shall never ask), the most comforting end to the sorrow that seems so comfortless now, the most beautiful end to our story, the most glorious of new beginnings—all this will be, "If it were not so I would have told you."

Sometimes there cannot be a glimmer of light on this side of time. The snapping of the delicate thread which we call reason can make a sunless gloom, but it cannot disannul the promises of God. "The Lord redeemeth the soul of His servants: and none of them that trust in Him shall be desolate" ("condemned," or "held guilty," as in the A.S.V. and marginal reading). The Septuagint of this verse (Psalm 34:22) says gently, *"None of them that hope in Him shall go wrong."*

For God sees the whole man, and He has a tender way of

looking at a soul at its highest, not its lowest. He does not do as we so often do, misjudge it because of what its diseased mind made its body do in a blind and broken hour. And our dealings are with a Love that can grasp the poor hands as they reach out to Him in that darkness—what father would not do that? And He is our Father.

But when those who have prayed for such a one have no assurance that there was ever any turning to Him who alone can save, then indeed we seem to be viewing a land like that hopeless country the prophet Isaiah describes, whose streams shall be turned into pitch, and the dust thereof into brimstone. "And He shall stretch out upon it the line of confusion and the stones of emptiness." But a word of peace comes through the confusion: prayer in the name of His Beloved Son does not fall upon stones of emptiness. Sometime, somewhere, we shall know better than we know now how gracious the Lord is. "Thy noblesse and infinite goodness ceaseth not to do well, yea, to the unkind and far turned away from Thee." Such thoughts do not tend to carelessness. Who could be careless about sin with Calvary in view? It is not by looking at sin that we see it for what it is, but by looking at the love of God and His pure holiness. As we look at *that* we begin to understand something of the texture and nature of sin.

5

"I have nigh forgotten this image; but now I return again thereto," says an old writer simply when he wanders a little. I have nigh forgotten the rough water, but now I return again thereto.

There is no question of deliverance from crossing that water. We follow One for whom there was no deliverance. "Now is my soul troubled; and what shall I say? Father, glorify Thy name." The petition is for deliverance *out of* and not for deliverance *from* the crisis of trial. So that the sense appears to be "Bring me safely out of the conflict," and not simply "Keep me from entering into it"—this interpretation has often brought illumination and peace. With it tallies Rotherham's rendering of Psalm 55:18, "He hath completely redeemed my soul out of the attack upon me."

Before we reach the place where such waters must be crossed, there is almost always a private word spoken by the Beloved to the lover. That is the word which will be most assaulted as we stand within sight and sound of that seething, roaring flood. The enemy will fasten upon it, twist it about, belittle it, obscure it, try to undermine our confidence in its integrity, and to wreck our tranquility by making us afraid, but this will put him to flight: *I believe God that it shall be even as it was told me.*

For "Faith reaches out to what it does not grasp"; it is always saying, "Even now, Even there, Even so." But I know that even now that which is beyond human hope can be. I know that "even there, in the uttermost places, shall Thy hand lead me and Thy right hand shall hold me." And most tender, most intimate of all, "Even so, Father, for so it seemeth good in Thy sight." And here, as we know, "Even so" means simply "Yes." "Yes, Father," yes to everything, to every challenge of faith, to every mystery. And then, before we are aware, we have crossed the waters and they did not overflow us. And we look up, and away beyond, and high above us, like a finger pointing up into the sky, is the summit of a mountain, the mountain—our hearts tell us so— that is set for us to climb.

8

The Shining Summit

1

FOR us to climb—who are we that we should hope to climb? What is man, "this weed which a sunbeam withers"? And yet he must climb or perish. He could stay in the but within sight of the peak, walk in the path with the mountain in view, sit on the rocks on the bank and gaze at ease at that upsoaring beautiful thing, and enjoy it without stirring a yard, without an ache, or a strain, or a dazed, parched minute. But that would not be life. To grovel is not to live. "The whitest, purest, holiest heights of the spirit" call us, and will not be refused. We are deaf adders indeed if we do not hear that call.

After Everest and the giants of the earth, the Matterhorn may look small, but that mountain is no hillock, and many a man has seen it as a finger pointing steadfastly upward. Little ends and low imaginations cannot live in the presence of that white pyramid.

For "Love will be above, not detained with any low things"; her prayer is always to be set free from every detaining desire and reluctance; and she sees in each new day "the day of the grace of God that brings for us the discipline of renunciation,"[7] the renunciation of the runner who lays aside every weight, stripping from himself all that would hinder his race.

This discipline appears in many forms.

The scholar had hoped to add a few grains to the precious heap of the world's knowledge, but the demands of life leave no time for that. The loving heart had hoped to lighten many burdens, but illness or poverty sweeps that hope away. Still more private hopes had been cherished; these must be laid aside, and now it has nothing to give but love. It often happens that the Christian is asked to renounce the things that were his meat and marrow. And he is not told why. "The lover lost a jewel which he greatly prized, and was sorely distressed, until his Beloved put to him this question: 'Which profiteth thee more, the jewel that thou hadst or thy patience in all the acts of thy Beloved?'"

And there is for some a discipline of renunciation of natural desires in the daily acceptance of deprivations of various kinds, and in peacefulness in crippled conditions, limitations and frustrations, such as St. Paul's when he was the Lord's bondman. And there is that inner renunciation of the will in very little things, which no eye sees but God's.

It is to this discipline of renunciation that we are called, if indeed our hearts are set on the heights; and there must be no complaining in our streets. The word is always *Unto all patience and longsuffering with joyfulness*—there we see the shining summit clear against the sky. "For if there had been anything more better or more profitable to man than to suffer, Christ would verily have showed it by word and example. Drink the chalice of our Lord affectionately, if thou desire to be His friend and to have part with Him. Consolations commit to God; do He therewith as it pleaseth Him."

There comes a time when the personal falls from us and we cease from the weariness of being entangled and encumbered in ourselves, and do with all our hearts desire to be perpetually lifted up in spirit above ourselves. But the trouble of a loved one can throw us into a fever of agitation. And yet to lose our peace is to lose our power to help. The energies which might have been turned to power are wasted in effectless grieving. Our very thoughts by their teasing reiteration, like low, eager voices that will not stop talking, tire us out.

> Were half the breath so vainly spent,
> To heaven in supplication sent,
> Thy thankful cry would oftener be,
> "See what the Lord has done for me."

The simple words of this Olney hymn cling to memory when greater are forgotten.

If we are to pray we must turn from fear and turmoil. Job could do nothing for his friends until his own heart was at rest. In one sense, there can be no peace while anything on earth is sinful or suffers:

> Earth, heaven shall pass away
> Ere for your passionless peace we pray,
> Are ye deaf to the trumpets that call us today?
> Blind to the blazing swords?

But there is a peace that must be ours if we are to prevail. "Peace I leave with you, My peace I give unto you: not as the world giveth, give I unto you. Let not your heart be troubled, neither let it be afraid." The peace of our Lord Jesus was never a passionless peace.

2

Before that peace can be ours—the peace that truly passeth all understanding, for who can understand how it can be at all?—there must be a renunciation of faithless anxiety. To ask for that seems to be asking for the impossible. The father of the family is ill. He thinks of wife and children; his whole being is keyed to one intense desire to be well, to be with them. The mother is ill; her heart cries out to fly to her children and gather them under her wings. The bread-earner, caring for widowed mother and sisters, is disabled; would he not be heartless if he were at peace? The son or daughter pledged to the Master's business in a distant land has letters telling of need at home, and is crushed and torn. The child all but saved is swept off by a dark wave. Prayer is agony then. How can there be any peace? The convert is sucked back into the pit, and the heart that loved is broken. But life will suggest only too many illustrations of griefs which can come down like an avalanche over the soul and bury it in debris. It is far then from its mountain peak.

I do not know of any way of escape from that debris so swift and so certain as to ask oneself the question the angel Uriel asked the prophet Esdras, *"Lovest thou that people better than He that made them?"* That question sounds the depths. There is a melting tenderness in it too, that prepares us for the beautiful words that follow, when the messenger seems to lose himself in his message, so that we hear a Greater than angels speak:

"Number Me them that are not yet come, gather Me together the drops that are scattered abroad, make Me the flowers green again that are withered, open Me the chambers that are closed, and bring Me forth the winds that in them are shut up, or show Me the image of a voice: and then I will declare to thee the travail that thou seekest to see. . . . Like as thou canst do none of these things that I have spoken of even so canst thou not find out My judgment, or the end of the love that I have promised unto My people. . . . In the beginning, when the earth was made, before the outgoings of the world were fixed . . . then did I consider these things, and they all were made through Me alone, and through none other: as by Me also they shall be ended, and by none other."

This is not Holy Scripture, but it is wisdom whose price is above rubies. *Lovest thou thy beloved better than He that made them?* Trust My love for thy beloved.

3

The hills of South India drop steeply towards the Indian Ocean. From the high rocks where the ibex find safe foothold you can see the waves that continually wash up in vast quantities two kinds of magnetic sand, monazite and ilmenite. Monazite is composed largely of thorium (the name looks back to the Scandinavian Thor) and is used in making incandescent gas mantles. It glistens, but is of a dull color. The pure thorium oxide is extracted from ilmenite and is used as the finest pigment in white paint and enamel. Ilmenite is black. The valuable sand is separated from the other sand (which looks far more valuable, for it often seems all garnet and crystal and jacinth) first by magnet, and finally by vibrating tables down which it is run, and where the magnetic impurities are separated out by gravity.

The process of water-grinding in the sea (by which the particles of ore are detached from the original rock), friction of grain upon grain in the rough and tumble of the waves, the influence of a force which we name and use but cannot explain, the tedious, tiny agitations of the vibrating cables, which call into effective co-operation the mighty pull of the earth—all these processes work together to bring forth from a black sand whiteness, and from a dull-colored sand a substance which helps towards illumination.

And the first of these is the breaking up of the rock in the bed of the sea; the discipline of renunciation. It is a figure of the true. First the severance: that which is death to the old order of being, then many a blow that we call blinding, little unexplained constraints, tedious minutes of shifting circumstance—that out of mere dust of earth something good may be prepared for the use of Him whom we call master and Lord.

And all this is part of the preparation for the spiritual climb.

It is true that "for a man never to feel trouble, nor suffer heaviness in body nor in soul, is not the state of this world, but the state of everlasting quiet," and yet it is possible to cast all our care on our Lord or we should not be told to do so. And sometimes the cares are so many and so heavy that if we did not cast them we could not bear up at all. The one way, then, is the old way—"Casting all your care upon Him; for He careth for you."

He who asks us to do this knew what it was to be taunted about a burden. In that old book of close-packed riches, William Kay's *Psalms with Notes*, the opening phrase of Psalm 22:8 is translated *"Roll it on the Lord."* The notes state: "The mockers taunt the Sufferer with a phrase He had been in the habit of using. He has at last, they mean, an opportunity of testing His maxim." There may be some faint shadow of this which He endured appointed for us. We may be with those who do not understand. If so it will draw us closer to our Lord, who was not understood.

And now, Roll the burden of cares of thy life's way upon the Lord. *Cause it to go*, the Hebrew says; a push will do it. Cast thy care, *hurl* it—so the word is there. Hurl it with a forceful act of will: it is not enough to think of doing it. *Do* it. The three verbs seem to be chosen to bring home to us that this committal is a definite act. We do not glide into it. (We never do glide into any act of faith.) And the marginal reading which Young adopts, "Cast on Jehovah that which He hath given thee," carries us further still. The burden has not come of itself. It is a gift, a trust. If we deal with it as we are told we may, we shall find rest unto our souls.

In his note on our Lord's word about the illness of Lazarus, Westcott opens a very heaven of joy: "This sickness is not unto death (as its issue and end) but for—to serve and to advance—the glory of God, in order that the Son of God may be glorified thereby. In every other place in St. John the preposition used here marks the notion of 'sacrifice in behalf of'; and this idea lies under the narrative here. *There was some mysterious sense in which the sick man suffered in behalf of God's glory, and was not merely a passive instrument."*

These words touch more than illness of the body. If only we allow them to sink deep into our being, if only we refuse forbidding feelings and believe that even to us this grace is given, we shall indeed find rest.

In that rest we shall climb. The unrestful cannot climb. They are too busy adjusting and readjusting their burdens to have breath or strength to spare for such ascents.

9

Expose Yourself

1

"Expose yourself to the circumstances of His choice."

This little phrase, which has stood by many a climbing soul, seems to have been coined for our picture of great circumstances.

The confusion of the skies has been so wonderfully captured that we all but see the movement and hear the wind that rushes past. The cloud in the picture is sunlit, but with an awful speed it may cover the face of the mountain with darkness. Mist, rain, snow—the cloud may bring them all, and the precipice falls away at our feet. "But none of these things move me, neither count I my life dear unto myself, so that I might finish my course with joy"—there speaks the spiritual mountaineer.

No parable shows everything: no climber among the precipices purposely exposes himself to stormy wind, and he does not willingly walk into cloud. But spiritual mountaineers must; and at such an hour there must be "some perseverance when we are tired, some resoluteness not to let ourselves off easily," something akin to the spirit of the world's mountaineers, "a spirit firm and tenacious and ambitious enough to drive on the body to its seemingly last extremity." There is no such thing as an easy or a sheltered climb. But "what know they of harbors who toss not on the sea?" And what know they of succor who have never ventured in difficult places? We shall press through the mist and the smothering snow; we shall climb and not give way; for there is One Invisible with us, "and with every call of every hour His word is, let us go hence.'"

"*Us*": and we take this word in faith, just as we take such words as "The angel of the Lord encampeth round about them that fear Him and delivereth them," in faith. But the line between the seen and the unseen is as narrow as ever it was (a line is without breadth)—and even now, at times, God does as He did when He opened the eyes of the young man and he saw; and behold the mountain was full of horses and chariots of fire round about Elisha. Why should it not be so? The powers of the Eternal are not bound between the covers of His Book.

If there be something which appears to explain this flash of spiritual awareness, it is discredited and called "illusion." But he who was made aware of the presence of Another, an Unseen Companion, in some hour of supreme need, very humbly but very surely knows that it was no illusion. He speaks of his experience with diffidence (because so few will understand), but never with uncertainty.

But the call is to the walk of faith, for we walk by faith, not by sight. (It would be sight if our spiritual senses were constantly quickened so that like that young man at Dothan we "saw.") And as we "go hence," refusing no roughness, no steepness, no danger, and caring not at all what the weather is, or what it threatens to be, we know that we are not alone on the mountain.

2

"Cast not away therefore your confidence, which hath great recompense of reward." Cast it not away when Grief is a companion with whom you must learn to become acquainted—

"Acquainted with grief": the words are real now.

Two friends are bound together in love; the call to go to a foreign land for Christ comes to one; it does not come to the other. There must be renunciation then, or eternal loss.

Or something even more poignant happens. Both hear the call, one goes abroad. The other prepares to follow. But the providence of God holds that one at home. Constraint that nothing can weaken holds the other abroad. Who can measure spiritual pain? Who can weigh the exceeding and eternal weight of glory that is being wrought while the eyes of faith are fixed, not on the pain, but on that which lies beyond it? But of this good thing they see nothing yet, not even the shadow. They only know they will not serve their Lord together now.

Very tender comforts are prepared for such as these. They will find them as they go on.

But theirs is a pure sorrow. It is not touched by the soiled fingers of earth. Some find themselves in the midst of clouds and darkness because of the sinful deeds of others. And yet the wrongdoing of another should have no power to darken the way of a child of God. At such times our peace is found in believing that things that are not good can be caused to work together for good. They are all subject to Him whose works are very great and whose thoughts are very deep. "There is no mist over His eyes who is wonderful in counsel."

The same word is comfort if the trouble be the result of our own doing. A wrong turning was taken at the foot of the hill. A wrong decision was made which has affected the whole course of life. The husband has been handicapped by a wife who can never enter into his deepest thoughts. The wife has been held from the highest she knew by the husband whose eyes were on the plains. Divided counsels in the bringing up of children tell upon the children. That means sorrow.

These circumstances were not the choice of God for those

lives, but it is impossible to go back and begin again, and each day will bring its trials of patience and its private griefs.

View all this as a glorious chance to prove the power of your God to keep you in peace and in hope and in sweetness of spirit. In that sense "expose yourself" to those circumstances. Do not fret against them. Do not fret by a dour countenance those who cause them to be. *"Beloved, let us love"* is a wonderful word for such difficult situations. And love is happy, not dour.

Even if you seem to be pushing through some long-trailing wisp of cloud, like that which lies on the face of the Matterhorn, be of good cheer. Your God has not forsaken you. He has not said, "Ephraim is joined to idols: let him alone"; a heart "let alone" feels nothing. Rather, indeed, the clouds are comforting: "Is my gloom, after all, the shade of His hand, outstretched caressingly?" It was when He was coming to the relief of His servant that He was seen upon the wings of the wind, and He made darkness pavilions round about Him—even dark waters, and thick clouds of the skies (Psalm 18:11). So clouds assure us of His presence; for where pavilions are spread, there the King dwelleth.

Often we find ourselves in precipitous, perhaps cloudy places because of some act of obedience. Such acts are called "ventures of faith," but there is no venture where faith is concerned. We walk on rock, not on quicksand, when we obey. But there is no promise that the rock will be a leveled path, or like the carpet of roses that Cleopatra spread for the officers of Mark Antony.

Sooner or later God meets every trusting child who is following Him up the mountain and says, "Now prove that you believe this that you have told Me you believe, and that you have taught others to believe." Then is your opportunity. God knows, and you know, that there was always a hope in your heart that a certain way would not be yours. "Anything but that, Lord," had been your earnest prayer. And then, perhaps quite suddenly, you found your feet set on that way, that and no other. Do you still hold fast to your faith that He maketh your way perfect?

It does not look perfect. It looks like a road that has lost its sense of direction: a broken road, a wandering road, a strange mistake. And yet, either it is perfect, or all that you have believed crumbles like a rope of sand in your hands. There is no middle choice between faith and despair.

3

There are flying vapors that are not the sign of His presence. Every worker for God knows this. Ours "the mighty ordination of the pierced Hands," but the long months before a missionary has liberty to speak in a new tongue can cause him to slip into a dullness that can cling like a wet mist. Shocks of disillusionment, numbing disappointments, can chill, and continually there may be something like the dropping of ice water, drop by drop, on the warm heart. The enemy sees to that. It is possible to be almost content to offer dead things, nothings, shams,

> Dead ashes, husk of corn for wheat—
>   Lord of our Ordination vow,
> We gather round Thy wounded feet,
>   We see the thorns about Thy brow.
>
> Now by Thy cross and passion, Lord,
>   Grant us this plea, this sovereign plea:
> Save us from choosing peace for sword,
>   And give us souls to give to Thee.

Life is a journey; it is a climb; it is also and always a war. The soldier of the Lord of Hosts is always a soldier. He dare not drivel down to any other kind of life. This sounds a rough word, but sometimes roughness helps. When a liquid has got past its boiling temperature, and yet will not boil, if a lead shot or anything with a roughened surface, which will carry down a few minute bubbles of air, be dropped into it, the boiling begins at once.

Apollos the Alexandrian had a spirit that boiled (*fervent*, to boil, be hot). Alexandria did not then, any more than it does now, encourage fervency of spirit. But there is no place where the soldier of the King of kings need be a simmering weakling. The soldier who simmers, but does not boil, is no soldier. He is a sham. Of all the futile figures on the battlefield he is the most futile.

May God take this true word, this small rough word (like the rough lead shot) and drop it into some heart that "will not boil"; and may the Breath of Life cause the boiling to begin at once. God multiply Apollos.

It is the keen Apollos who most feels the long delays in fruition, as he finds "the exercise of hope a more difficult and expensive duty" than he ever imagined it would be. It is he who is most tempted to discouragement when he sees so many who can look no way but downward, and spend their time raking to themselves the straws, the small sticks and dust of the floor, though there stands One who proffers a crown for the muckrake. The world seems full of muckrakes and of people who diligently use them. Heaven is but as a fable to such, and things here are counted the only things substantial. How can the good seed lodge in hearts so occupied, so dulled? He asks himself this question again and again. And yet he has our Lord's sure promise that labor in Him is not in vain, the sower shall doubtless return with rejoicing, bringing his sheaves with him. Many a sower has thanked God for these two words, "shall doubtless."

4

There are two notable effects of light in this part of South India. One is seen on a clear evening when the terra-cotta earth of the plains, and every brick and tile made of that earth, takes on a brief and amazing brightness. The other is still more fugitive.

It is never seen except in thundery weather, and then only on the hills that run down the western coast like a spine set out of place. The sun's rays striking up from the sea in sunrise are flung back by the thundercloud, and falling on mountain and forest turn the whole world to rose. The loveliness of such moments is unearthly. You stand speechless on some rock in the heart of that celestial rose. You can only worship. Worthy, worthy to be worshiped is the God who can imagine such beauty and command it. All your soul worships. Be still and know that I am God.

The beauty passes. The rose light melts into the light of day, and in this it is a figure of the truth. There are certain glories that are brief, like those lovely lights, but there is the common sunlight that is the life of every day. We live far too little in this light of life. What a witness to the world Christians would be if only they were more evidently very happy people. "There be many that say, 'Who will show us any good?' Lord, lift Thou up the light of Thy countenance upon us." If we lived in the light of that Countenance, continually filled by the God of Hope with all joy and peace in believing, the dreary question "Who will show us any good?" would be answered.

In my copy of that missionary classic *On the Threshold of Central Africa* I keep a letter from C.W. Mackintosh, who edited the Journals and wrote the life of her uncle, M. Coillard. "I often think of your title 'Overweights of Joy' (from St. Paul's 'I have more than an overweight of joy'). The joy of the Lord is your strength. The saints are full of it, even when cast down and oppressed by circumstances. Love and joy breathed from them, and everybody felt they had a blessed secret to impart. I don't think anything else but this can make much headway among the heathen, for the offer of pardon can only appeal to the sense of sin which most of them have not got. So Satan's great efforts are to offer the world a substitute for that joy, and to deprive us of it. Do you know that saying (I think, of J.G. Belletes), 'There is nothing puts such a lever under the soul as the sense that God's favor is towards us'? Oh, the joy of meeting an unrebuking gaze!"

Thunderclouds are nothing to the Spirit of Joy. The only special reference to the joy of the Holy Spirit is bound up with the words "much affliction," much pressure. It is the rose under thundercloud again.

"Joy is not gush: joy is not jolliness. Joy is simply perfect acquiescence in God's will, because the soul delights itself in God Himself. Christ took God as His God and Father, and that brought Him at last to say, 'I delight to do Thy will,' though the cup was the cross, in such agony as no man knew. It cost Him blood. It cost Him blood. O take the Fatherhood of God in the blessed Son the Saviour, and by the Holy Ghost rejoice, rejoice in the will of God, and in nothing else. Bow down your heads and your hearts before God, and let the will, the blessed will of God, be done."

These weighty words were spoken by Prebendary Webb-Peploe to a gathering of Christians many years ago. In the silence that closed the hour, the speaker—some knew it—was laying, not for the first time, his Isaac on the altar of his God. It is the life lived that gives force to the words spoken. These words were not wind and froth. They sound through the years like the deep notes of a bell: *"Joy is not gush: joy is not jolliness. Joy is perfect acquiescence in the will of God."*

This, then, is the call to the climbing soul. Expose yourself to the circumstances of His choice, for that is perfect acquiescence in the will of God. We are called to the fellowship of a gallant company. "Ye became followers of us, and of the Lord," wrote St. Paul to the men of Thessalonica. Who follows in their train?

Make me Thy mountaineer—
I would not linger on the lower slope.
Fill me afresh with hope, O God of hope,
That undefeated I may climb the hill

As seeing Him who is invisible,
 Whom having not seen I love.
O my Redeemer, when this little while
Lies far behind me and the last defile
Is all alight, and in that light I see
My Saviour and my Lord, what will it be?

10

Edelweiss

1

THE mountains bring to mind little simple things—flowers. If any ask, "How has the climber, whose whole thought is set upon the heights, time to stop and look for flowers?" I can only answer in the words of *The Imitation*, "If thou withdraw thyself from void speaking and idle circuits, and from vanities and hearing of tidings, thou shalt find time sufficient and convenient for to have sweet meditations and discoveries." Sweet meditations and discoveries are the peculiar treasure of mountaineers. And they always find, I think, that far more than the toils of the climb, they remember the places where they gathered the edelweiss of God.

A chance reminder of the Spiritual may bring this peculiar treasure: the Sign of our faith (unpremeditated) in the woodwork of a door, a window, a roof. You may find it, perhaps, in common wire netting. You see the wire if you "look through" it casually: you are conscious of it, even though not looking at it. But if you focus intently on something beyond you hardly see it; and if you have field glasses you do not see it at all. (Lord, evermore give it us to look intently through the field glasses of faith.)

Or it may be something even less obvious, which has a word for our heart that it has not for any other at that moment: the coming of some Ebed-melech, a letter, a book. "Having so many

and so great causes for joy, he is very much in love with sorrow
and peevishness who loses all these pleasures, and chooses to sit
down on his little handful of thorns."

For some, the flowers of God take the form of music or a
song: "And is that the great Dr. George Matheson?" asked a
disillusioned child, as she gazed astonished at the blind minister,
writer of hymns and neat brown books out of which her mother
sometimes read to her pages that somehow were not dull. He
was dining at the time—just dining. The child had revered
him because he was so courageous; he had refused to let the
blindness that had slowly crept upon him hinder, and his "O
Love that will not let me go" had said far more to her than she
could understand. She had thought of him as almost in heaven,
and there he was, at an ordinary dinner table, and apparently
enjoying what he ate. This last was quite a shock. It was years
before that secular dinner table settled itself comfortably in her
mind, and she knew his song for what it truly was, his edelweiss
found for his consolation on his dark Matterhorn.

But probably we do not feel in the least like George
Matheson or any of the noble clan of climbers who conquered
gloriously and sang gloriously too. Does it matter? God knows
all about that. To one of no account, who did not feel able to
bring anything worth offering, a sweet and gentle comfort came
through the moonlight that was shining on the grass and trees.
It was only silver, not like the glory of the morning gold. "Offer
thy silver," said a quiet voice. And peace came that moonlit night
in offering just silver:

> I cannot bring Thee praise like golden noon-light
>   Shining on earth's green floor.
> My song is more like silver of the moonlight,
>   But I adore.
>
> I cannot bring Thee, O Beloved, ever
>   Pure song of woodland bird;

And yet I know the song of Thy least lover
   In love is heard.

O blessed be the love that nothing spurneth:
   We sing—Love doth enfold
Our little song in love. Our silver turneth
   To fine-spun gold.

2

I have read that when the Spanish adventurers looked across the St. Lawrence and saw the unexplored land north of that river they thought it was of no account. And so they wrote Aca Naia (Canada), "Here is nothing," upon their maps.[8] Our God does not write on the map of our lives, "Here is nothing." He sees much. He sees that map set with snowfields, woods, waters, mountains, plains. There can be no difficulty of travel that He does not understand. We are never alone as we penetrate the unknown. We cannot be lost there. It does sometimes seem almost unbelievable that the soul of man can pass through so many devastating experiences and yet not be devastated. The explanation lies in such words as these: "He knoweth the way that I take."

But strewn among the big and really shattering things there are often tiresome trifles that can seem quite important and draw attention to themselves. And yet, "They are gone! Why write their epitaph?" This saying (it is a kind of little laughing edelweiss) dates from an ancient Keswick convention. The meetings were over and the speakers were departing. The coach, piled up with luggage, was ready to start, when there was a cry for Theodore Monod of Paris, who was to leave by that coach and who had disappeared; so the youngest in the house was dispatched posthaste to call him. She raced upstairs and found him sitting at a round table, eyes screwed up, forehead wrinkled, left hand tugging distractedly at a lanky lock of hair, right hand flourishing a pencil. He was counting aloud in a great hurry, *"Un, deux, trois, quatre, cinq,"* then, glancing at the messenger as she stood in the doorway, "Always one counts in one's mother tongue." So she knew that he was busy with his petty cash, and he had her sympathy, when, after a minute of desperate scribbling, he stopped. "It is gone! Why write its epitaph?" As a rule to be applied to accounts it may not be approved, but as a way of dealing with the little ills of life it is excellent; a bad night, a bad day, a worry, a small pain, a petty annoyance. It is gone. Why write its epitaph?

Why indeed? "A good thing from David today," writes the father of five-year-old David Somervell. "Out of the mouth of babes: When climbing a little hill with me he said, puffing and blowing, but going very strong, 'Nannie always says she wants to stop and get her breath when she's climbing up a hill, but I don't—I only think of getting to the top.'" It is when we stop to "get our breath" that we have time to write epitaphs of past troubles. The best way is little David's as he climbs his infant Everests, "I only think of getting to the top."

And if "the top" means for the reader peace in some long trial of patience and of faith, perhaps this from another letter will be an edelweiss: "Oda has just brought in the verse on her French calendar for today, Proverbs 24:14: 'Know wisdom for thy soul; if thou hast found it, then there is a future, and thy waiting shall not be reduced to nothing, or be in vain.'" And a letter, quoting a recent *Times*, adds a flower to the cluster: "The grace of final perseverance is that quality of patience which is always equal to the pressure of the passing moment, because it is rooted in that eternal order over which the passing moment has no power."

Those trifles which may not be worth an epitaph will either help or hinder as they pass and touch us with small casual fingers. We have an Indian fern whose frond changes as it grows. As the forces of life play upon it and work within it, each little pinna divides and subdivides till, in the end, the frond is a fan of delicate lace, a feathery fan.

"What has been the effect upon him of all the trouble?" we asked a guest who had been telling us of her father, and of how he had suffered from injustice. "It has left him unable to think an unkind thought of anyone," she answered. The frond of that fern had been perfected.

If the wear and tear of life on a soul does not make for beauty, the process of the fern is reversed. The multitude of insignificant, trying things that are sure to come fret it into a ragged selfishness; and rough blows coarsen its texture. Or if it be otherwise fashioned it reacts to the touch like a jarred sea anemone, gathering itself within itself. Then (unlike the anemone, which, if left in peace, opens again) the jarred soul gradually closes completely, and hardens, till it acquires the power to jar others even as it was jarred. So there is loss. Fellow lovers, who were meant to meet, pass each other coldly. They do not even recognize each other as members of one family. Each is frozen in his own ice. But the love of God shed abroad in our hearts (not filtered through various screens) can melt us and love us out of fretfulness, and out of hardness. It was said of one who lived this life, "Love gladdened him. Love quickened him. Love set him free." Love sets us free to love. And having been set free it is impossible to be bound any more.

3

The words of our Lord are often swords quick and powerful and sharper than any two-edged sword. Sometimes they are pearls, sometimes seed pearls, easily overlooked, but how beautiful when found. His words about the candle, "and it giveth light unto all that are in the house," are precious seed pearls. The candlelight will shine through the windows on the people who pass in the street, but it has first lighted all who are in the house.

When candles are so arranged that their light is chiefly for the street, there is sure to be fret for the people in the house. But even this can be turned to heavenly uses.

In a certain Indian hospital there was at one time a candle whose light may have been directed to the world out of doors but certainly did not shine much on the indoor folk. And for them life was sometimes difficult. One day something was said to a younger helper which all but drew forth a flashing retort. At that moment this came: *"See in it a chance to die."* The word was spoken inwardly, but it was far more clearly heard than many a word addressed to the outward ear. See in it—in this provoking, in this that should not have been—a chance to die to self and the pride of self, to that in you which would strike in self-defence. See in anything that rouses you to claim your "rights," even to see them or to consider them at all, *see in it* a chance to die. Welcome anything that calls you to your only true position, "I am crucified with Christ."

A crucified life cannot be self-assertive. It cannot protect itself. It cannot be startled into resentful words. The cup that is full of sweetness cannot spill bitter drops however sharply knocked. *Lord, fill my cup with sweetness. Keep very far from me the juice of the gall*—to be brought to that prayer is to be blessed by the flowers of God on our mountain.

Often our edelweiss is an enriching friendship: "For every guest thy heart receiveth, the Lord Himself doth open in thy heart another room. It is as if Christ handed to us Himself the key of each newly discovered chamber, saying, 'Let us together love to the best end, the dear soul who enters here.' As love grows we discover further and further the capacity of the house of our soul. There is no limit to the number or kind of 'these My brethren,' to whom we give the freedom of this city without walls."

And there is no limit to love. We were never meant to be

like a pool of water which grows just a little shallower with every pebble dropped into it. A city of many houses, a house with many rooms—that is what we are meant to be. The rooms do not impinge on one another; they grow, each a perfect thing, like the cell of a honeybee in the comb. And to each friend is a cell into which no other ever enters. For as in Aaron's breastplate each precious stone had a name engraved upon it, each set in an "inclosing" of gold, "And they shall be upon Aaron's heart when he goeth in before the Lord," so it is with the jewels of friendship: each several jewel has its name engraved upon it, each is set in its golden inclosing, and they are all upon our heart when we go in before the Lord.

New guests welcomed into our city without walls, new precious stones, new powers of loving—those are among the starriest flowers to be found on any Matterhorn.

4

A difficult decision, the kind that looks like sheer cliff, can lead straight to where the flowers of light, as someone has called them, grow up and down the rocks. "The work of righteousness shall be peace; the effect of righteousness quietness and assurance for ever." However trying to flesh and blood the right act may be, once hesitation is over and the way is clearly seen, then the effects begin to appear: peace, quietness, assurance forever.

What would be called loneliness by those who do not know the secret of the Lord can turn into an angel's garden on the face of the cliff. With many other climbers I have found such gardens.

There was a year a long time ago, before our Indian family as it is now had been created, when I had to be left alone, because illness had forced my fellow missionaries to go home on furlough. It was a year of edelweiss.

That year began in the hour when I stood on the verandah

of our three-roomed bungalow, listening to the scrunch of the wheels of the bullock cart as it turned on the rough gravel and drove unwillingly away. The cry of a child in delirium seemed to fill the house (for a little girl I was nursing was very ill: she almost died that night). There was no one else in the house. The servants had gone to their homes in the village, the Indian woman who would presently help me had not come yet; the rooms had that forlorn, deserted air that rooms always wear just after their owners have gone, but I was not lonely. There was something new in the "feel" of the house, familiar and yet new, and that sense of a light in a dim place, and an infinitely loving, brooding Presence near (but "near" is too distant a word) was an abiding strength.

But I know it is not the sense of His presence, it is the *fact* of His presence that is our strength and stay. And yet it is comforting when a mother makes some little sign, or speaks some little word to a child who does not see her. And when our Father deals so tenderly with us, then we are very humbly grateful and we store such memories in our heart. And when there is not any feeling we rest on His bare word, "Lo, I am with you always, all the days, and all day long," and are content.

The bright flowers of the edelweiss waiting to be gathered among the rough rocks of difficult circumstances—we may call the consolations of God what we will—who are we that we should find such comforts anywhere? Love prepared, Love planted, Love led us to these enchanting discoveries. A child cannot bear to enjoy a delight alone; it turns to its nearest friend with a shout of joy and shares its treasures. Turn so to thy Nearest, soul beloved, speak thy quick thanks and share thy joy. Forget not the Giver in the gift. Offer not the discourtesy of remembering thy Unseen Companion only when nettles sting thee, and thorns prick thee, and thy feet are cut on the stones.

11

The Land of Far Distances

1

OFTEN when our feet have been cut on the stones, and we are much tempted to think of these passing hurts, we turn a corner, and see outspread before our delighted eyes something so reviving and so beautiful that we forget about the travail of the way. It is with us then as it was with the young man in the Dothan story: our eyes are opened and we see what was already there before we saw it; just as sometimes our ear is quickened and we hear in a new way. Spiritual sense may be refined at any moment. We are not all and only flesh.

Something like this happens even on the earthly plane. If one to whom beauty is not merely form and color but the hem of the garment of God looks quietly and intently for a little while upon any lovely thing, he will presently see far more in it than he saw at first, and as he looks, thoughts beyond the reaches of our souls will disturb, or kindle, or delight him.

It was a touch of genius in John Bunyan that made him take his pilgrim to the top of the House Beautiful just after he had climbed the hill Difficulty, just before he met Apollyon, and long before he reached his journey's end. Even so did a greater John tell of a heavenly vision shown to him after he had climbed the steep hill of tribulation, before he fought a stern fight for the truth in a very evil age and many years before his race was over.

It has always been the custom of our Father to let us look into
heaven while the fogs of earth are about us. It is then that the
earthly ceases to dominate. We have seen something better than
that. And deep in our happy hearts we know that all that grieves
us is but for a moment, and all that pleases is but for a moment,
and only the eternal is important, as the words carved above the
doors of Milan Cathedral declare: "Let not the world deceive
me, and its short glory." These words have virtue in them. They
can still us when we look at the world, and even at the professing
church—that strange travesty of the spiritual, where men praise
him who does well to himself. There is not much happiness to
be found in looking at the shell of things. But the shell is not
the substance. All this that looks so important now is but for the
moment. Only the eternal is important. And everywhere under
the painted show God treasures the eternal.

On the wall of the guest room of a Rhenish Mission house in
Sumatra a guest saw a prayer, which he translated thus:

> Light of eternity, light divine,
> Into my darkness shine,
> *That the small may appear small,*
> *And the great, greatest of all:*
> O light of eternity, shine.

The beautiful German hymn, of which the above is the last
verse, is a prayer for common days: "Break forth, sweet shining
of divine light; illuminate our poor life; give strength to our feet,
joy to our souls. There is care in the early morning, care in the
late evening, fear, and heartbreaking trouble. Often a cold wind
blows. Jesus Christ, Thou alone art the light of our hope; come
forth and let us see Thy green pastures, the promise of Thy word.
Light of eternity, shine."

2

So we pray, and in answer to our prayer the blessed light is given. For light is like water (and like love); remove whatever forbids it, and nothing can hold it back.

But it can be only too easily forbidden. "Curious inquisition of other men's living" can forbid it: "Son, be not curious, nor be busy. What is this or that to thee? Follow thou Me. What is that to thee, whether such a man be such and such, or what this man doeth, or what he saith? Thou hast no need to answer for others, but for thyself thou must yield account." Indifference to the concern of others is equally forbidding. "Pour out Thy grace from above; wash my soul in that heavenly dew that I may be enlarged in vision." There is much happiness then, for we see the sunlight fall on all the trees of the forest, and this is better than only to see it fall on the one little cherished tree that we think of as our own.

Sometimes there is a peculiar joy in this. We may be set in a place where a conversion does not open doors to the gospel but closes them, perhaps for years. But elsewhere it is different. We may seem to be fighting a losing battle, but somewhere else they are winning. If we look out on the field which is the world there is always something to be glad about.

And in smaller matters it is the same. The things I cannot do, another can. The things I do poorly, another can do well. There is a peculiarly golden quality in this kind of joy. It fills the quiet spaces of the heart with singing.

But it may be broken by even a moment's occupation with self, for self is clamorous, and where that clamor is the air is too unquiet for songs. If like the Spanish traveler Ulloa and his friends, and like some of us on our Indian mountains—like the airman too, when he ascends high above the earth—we see the shadow of our own image in the circle that is flung upon the mist, then we see nothing else, hear nothing but the noisy talk

Selfish desire to be used.

of self. This "I" that is myself can disturb our very holiest things. The passionate longing (for it is indeed a passion and a pain) to be the one to rise and serve is the last thing to die in the heart that loves its fellows and finds its joy in serving them, just as the last prayer we drop is the prayer that we (with an emphasis on the we) may be used.

Is this a hard saying? But why? The pen on the desk is kept clean and filled with ink. The pencil is kept pointed. Both are ready, both are at hand; sometimes one is used, sometimes the other; if only the work be done, what does it matter which does it? There can be a subtle selfishness, a kind of covetousness which is idolatry (of self) in the perpetual cry, Use me.

But there is nothing of that in the prayer, "Cleanse me, O Lord, and keep me clean; make me sensitive to the approach of sin. Make me quick to hear Thy question, 'Whom shall I send?' and quick to answer, 'Here am I'; quick also to be glad if another be preferred before me." Nor is there anything selfish in such a prayer as this,

> Love through me, Love of God;
> Make me like Thy clear air
> That Thou dost pour Thy colors through,
> As though it were not there.

There is nothing of earth, thank God, in the soaring rapture of the winged words, "His servants shall serve Him: and they shall see His face; and His name shall be in their foreheads"—O joy beside which all joys pale, we welcome thee. We see thee drawing nearer, we almost hear thy footsteps, and we greet thee.

But there are days when the spirit, growing impatient, pushes far past the body's permissions and seems to spring out between its bars, and then is caught back and held fast again. And yet even then we know that when those bars fall and in the twinkling of an eye our mortal has put on immortality, nothing will matter to us but that in the brief waiting time we did not grieve the love that trusted us to wait.

And while we wait, as it seems in strict bondage, we are not bound, we are free; we are free as happy birds that never knew a cage. No bars can forbid the soul to soar: One thing have I desired of the Lord, that will I seek after; that I may dwell in the house of the Lord all the days of my life (not only afterwards but now, in this daily present), to behold the beauty of the Lord, and to enquire in His temple.

And, so I take it, we may understand the Jerusalem of that little old book *The Scale of Perfection* very simply. Today, in this prosaic today, surrounded by the common things of life, beset by its common temptations, pledged to its common duties, we may be at home in our Father's house; becoming, because of His patient work upon us, more and more like the children of that House, "ever thirsting and softly seeking" His blessed Presence so that others may be drawn to seek Him and with Him also continually dwell.

3

"And after this, when thine enemies see that thou art so well willed, then are they much abashed. But then will they assay thee with flattering and vain pleasing. Thus do thine enemies that thou shouldest think their saying sooth, and have delight in this vain joy and rest thee therein. But if thou do well, thou shalt hold all such jangling as falsehood and flattery of thine enemy, that proffereth thee to drink venom tempered with honey. And therefore refuse it and say thou wilt not thereof, but thou wouldest be at Jerusalem." "Thou art not there yet," says Hilton, in another place, "but by small sudden lightnings that glide out of small caves from that city shalt thou be able to see it from far ere that thou come thereto." And so indeed it is for us at times, to the comfort of our hearts.

But for him who would be at Jerusalem there is something

that can smite and pierce and humble in the vision of the rainbow shown to the prophet Ezekiel and to John the Evangelist.

When one rises high in our material air one sees the rainbow in full circle. And so it is in things heavenly. Rising high in the spiritual air those two most happy seers saw that same glory, the rainbow in full circle, but they did not see the shadow of themselves. As the appearance of the bow that is in the cloud in the day of rain, so was the appearance of the brightness round about the throne that they saw. Upon "the likeness of the throne was the likeness as the appearance of a Man"—thus Ezekiel. And St. John: "I beheld, and, lo, in the midst of the throne stood a Lamb as it had been slain."

Self nowhere, nothing; our Lord Christ in all things preeminent--we hunger and thirst for that. The mountains under the quiet sky would be nothing to us if they did not speak of a detachment and a purity like that. Again and again the temptation to wish for what is not given will spring upon us ("jangle not therewith"), and the staining, softening thought of self, and sympathy with self, will try to creep into the circle. But if the moment the soul is conscious of that influence it looks to its Lord ("I am naught, I have naught; I covet naught but only the love of Jesus") there will be peace; there will be victory. Not I, but Christ, will fill the center of the circle. And "He will with His merciful might of gracious presence break down this false image of love in thyself, till thou be some deal reformed to His likeness."

So let us be of good courage, for each hour brings the hour nearer when we shall behold His face in righteousness, and we shall be like Him, for we shall see Him as He is. *I shall be satisfied when awakened by a vision of Thee:* that is the word of the Lake of Thun, pictured at the beginning of this chapter.

4

And its last word, or so I thought, till the post brought a parcel of old books for giving away, and "by chance" opening one I read this: "A few years ago, sojourning by the beautiful shores of the Lake of Thun, during a genial September, I walked day by day in sight of the orchards which cover those green fields and hills and saw their manner of fruit-bearing. It was as if the root and branches in their perfect *rapport* conspired to push out the golden apples wherever there was wood to carry them. The trees were not fruit-bearing only, they were 'filled with fruit,' to the praise of that sun and soil."

These moments of vision that come (who can tell how? the wind bloweth where it listeth) are meant to be like sunshine on our trees. In the midst of a crowded day we are given almost a glimpse of the land of far distances, and we stand still, arrested on the road. What was it that blessed our eyes? And then we know, for the hush upon our spirit tells us what it was.

Or we are facing a crisis in life. Every hour of that day is etched in memory like an etching on ivory. We know then what it is to be rent. It is like the rending of living flesh from living flesh. It is more than that. We have no words for what it is. Till suddenly we look up and see—but what was it that we saw? Something that was not of earth. And that bright hour never fades for us. Years flow over it like water over gold. They do not dim its brightness.

But all this that "may better be known by experience than by any writing" is never granted for our comfort only, but for the ripening of the golden apples that should be on the trees wherever there is wood to carry them. We are inclined to be content when we have feelings of sweetness; but the Gardener of souls seeks not for feelings but for fruit, to the praise of His sun and soil.

I turned to the title page of the small blue book which had offered me this word about the apples, to find the date of its writing. It was the year when I stood, a girl of seventeen, on the sunny hillside that looks on the mountain smothered in soft masses of cloud; but I had never seen that book before.

By kindly touches like this upon our work our Lord encourages us to hope that we are about our Father's business, even we who can so poorly serve. And I thanked Him for bringing me this incident of long ago from the Lake of Thun to complete the message of this chapter. There is something eternal in the simplest things of the Spirit.

12

And Then
the Dark Wood Again

1

"UNDERSTANDEST thou what thou readest?"—so
Philip to the Ethiopian. Understandest thou what
thou seest?—so my thought, "running thither" to the
unknown fellow traveler who opens on this page, would ask.
For it may be I am mistaken in hoping that these figures of the
true will have a voice for others. And yet a wise book says, "A
picture may with more fancy convey a story to a man than a
plain narrative either in word or writing."

Perhaps this second wood may find the traveler startled or
depressed by a recurrence of some trial which he had thought
was well behind him. "I have not passed this way heretofore," he
had said to himself when he entered the first dark wood. "I shall
henceforth return no more that way." Nor does he, but perhaps
just after a clear vision of peace from some House Beautiful he
finds confronting him something very like the dark wood of
earlier days. It is in fact a further reach of that wood.

Here is one, perhaps an athlete, who has never been ill and
never contemplated illness. He has become the vassal of Eternal
Love. *Look, love, and follow.* Prince Charlie engraved this motto

on his seal when he came to call the clans to suffer and die for him. The words are engraved upon the life of this soldier who has looked, loved, and followed his Prince overseas. But his first year sees him handicapped by illness. He recovers, is struck down again, he who never was ill before. This repeated illness, battle wound though it be—so unexpected, so exhausting—can appear like a very dark wood. Battle wounds may sound heroic, but they do not feel so.

Or the dark wood may be that scorched and arid feeling that leaves the soul like our South Indian foothills in drought:

> Faint is the famished forest-green,
> And parched the pools of the ravine;
> The burning winds have blown away
> The soft blue mist of yesterday.
>
> The furry creatures of the wood
> Have fled and left a solitude.
> No song of merry, singing bird
> Or laughter of the stream is heard.
>
> • • •
>
> So, Lord my God, Thy child would be,
> If for one hour bereft of Thee.
> But Thy great fountains from afar
> Flow down to where Thy valleys are;
>
> And for the least is nourishment,
> Verdure and song and heart-content.
> For where Thou art, there all is well,
> Our Life of life, Immanuel.

How often we have known the flowings of those fountains: it is not our Lord's pleasure that His valleys should be dry. But sometimes we are kept waiting for a while. If that be so, our thirst "hath some nourishing virtue in it, and giveth sap to humility, and putteth an edge on hunger, and furnisheth a fair field to faith to put forth itself, and to exercise its fingers in gripping it seeth not what." *I will wait upon the Lord that hideth His face. I will look for Him.* I will not be discouraged even though I am not given "little overflowings of spiritual joy and sensible pleasures and delicacies in prayer." Ye seek Me because ye did eat of the loaves. He loves us to seek Him just for Himself.

But often He gives us loaves, or if a loaf would be too much, a crumb.

To one, terribly injured by a runaway horse, such a crumb was given in that difficult hour after the surgeon had done his work and there was nothing to do but lie still and endure. "As I lay with my head and neck between sandbags, helpless as an infant" (this was her story afterwards), "wondering about it all, I heard a voice say distinctly to me, 'You have often said to yourself and to others, *Naught but in love denied*. You have now to believe and receive, *Naught but in love permitted*.' It was just the word I needed."

After such a consoling word there is always the prayer that God calls a song. There may not be strength for anything that we would call singing, but the faintest little whispering prayer reaches our Father's ear as a song: for as His majesty is, so also is His mercy. This small inconspicuous word of comfort is like a little flower in a field of greater flowers. It grows somewhat out of sight, but it will fill our room with fragrance if we pluck it and take it home.[9]

2

A profound and recurrent weariness of spirit because of the repeated, though perhaps smaller, trials that beset us may become a second dark wood.

One day I was preparing a microscope slide for a class of children, to whom I was giving simple lessons in biology, when I saw something I had never seen before.

The oil emulsion and that tricky detail, the light, had been happily adjusted, so that the film of water under the high-power lens had the velvety darkness of the midnight sky, when suddenly I found myself looking at a skyful of stars. And all the stars were moving, but moving in a curious way. Not one went straight forward, nor did any move in circles, or in any ordered fashion. It was as though unseen forces were perpetually beating upon the illuminated particles and pushing them about. The whole field of vision appeared to be nothing but a sparkling confusion. Later I learned that I had stumbled unawares upon that phenomenon known as the Brownian movement. The stars were truly being beaten upon, first on one side, then on the other, by those invisible forces, the molecules in the water, and so each particle was caused to move in an irregular zigzag. That explained what I had seen, so far as it can be explained.

There are times when we seem to be caught in a kind of spiritual Brownian movement and are pushed about almost past endurance by multitudinous molecules. Trouble seems to be everywhere; we are so buffeted that we hardly know how to hope for anything so simple and direct as a straight course across the field of life, or any ordered movement, or peaceful fulfillment of purpose. We feel like the stars at the mercy of the molecules, and more than a little confused and overborne.

And yet for the children of the Father, whatever is must be among the all things that work together for good. And, so the wise tell us, if it were not for molecules we would have no blue skies.

But our greatest trouble may be that we are tired of wrestling with tireless powers, tired of the cumbrance and the burden and the strife, and long for something different. In the heat of the work and warfare we have said within ourselves, "Oh, for a day without distresses about souls, a day without anxieties!" We have almost reached the place where Moses was when he said in effect, "Am I responsible for the existence of these children that Thou shouldest say unto me, Carry them in thy bosom?" And yet we could not help doing that very thing because they were dear unto us.

And then we have been ashamed, for we remembered the Good Shepherd, who endured the contradiction of sinners to the end, who was never tired of loving, who laid down His life for the sheep. And we have known ourselves unworthy to be called His undershepherds. There is nothing so grievous to the man or woman whose supreme life-purpose is shepherd work as the discovery of loss of shepherd love. To seem to be what one is not—that is the last word in distress. It may be that a sudden shock of disappointment in one dearly loved, perhaps a cold ingratitude, has drained the heart dry. Not that we ask for gratitude, but that a lack of response is a chilling thing. After years of love, of breaking toil, to be met by this can pull down the soul to the dust.

> Deep unto deep, O Lord,
>   Crieth in me;
> Gathering strength I come,
>   Lord, unto Thee.
> Jesus of Calvary,
>   Smitten for me,
> Ask what Thou wilt, but give
>   Love to me.

That is our prayer then. Yes, let strength go, health, vigor, the keen edge of our blade which once gone can never return, let anything go, if only love be left.

There is a place where love can be renewed. "Now there was leaning on Jesus' bosom one of His disciples whom Jesus loved . . . there stood by the cross of Jesus the disciple whom He loved. Jesus saith, *I thirst*."

But more than pains that racked Him then
   Was the deep longing thirst divine
That thirsted for the souls of men:
   Dear Lord, and one was mine.

It was the disciple who leaned upon His breast and stood beside His cross who heard that word, "I thirst." Is it not always so? O Lord of Calvary, hold us so close to Thee that we shall be drawn into that fellowship, that thirst.

This prayer goes very deep. It is not a light thing to ask to share in the fellowship of His sufferings, which is the fellowship of His love and of His thirst. "He that is not ready to suffer all things and to stand at the will of his Beloved is not worthy to be called a lover." We know we are not worthy. Such a life is like that knowledge which "is too high for me. I cannot attain unto it." We cannot attain; but when the Most High stoops to us who are low and fills us with the power of His life, then nothing is impossible. It is not that we attain. It is that He in us does that which we could never do.

We find this comforting truth in the parable of the Vine: *Abide in Me and I in you.* We have it in that figure of the true, the burning bush: "And the angel of the Lord appeared unto him in a flame of fire out of the midst of a bush: and he looked, and, behold, the bush burned with fire, and the bush was not consumed." The angel of the Lord did not choose the tall date palm of the Arabian oasis, which would have burned for hours like a glorious fiery torch. He chose the common low thorn of the desert which, set alight, burns up in a few minutes. There is nothing left of it then but a heap of ashes, soon to be blown away by the wind. It was this insignificance that He chose. God loves the "things that are not." We cannot be less than that. We cannot be less than an empty cockle shell lying on the beach. But the sea can flow over that shell and fill it full. It can be filled with all the fullness of the sea.

3

But the dark wood may be something quite different. It may be an exposure to a sudden temptation, perhaps connected in some subtle way with the very work itself—the work across which we have written "Holiness unto the Lord." If this be so, the tempter is sure to choose a weary hour, perhaps a discouraged hour. And he flings himself upon us with a violence unimagined before. But all the great staining temptations, to selfishness, ambition, and other strong sins that violently affront the soul, appear first in the region of the mind, and can be fought and conquered there. We have been given the power to close the door of the mind. We can lose this power through disuse or increase it by use, by the daily discipline of the inner man in things which seem small and by reliance upon the word of the Spirit of Truth. "It is God which worketh in you both to will and to do of His good pleasure." It is as though He said, Learn to live in your will, not in your feelings. Will to banish that evil thing, that thought, that imagination, and I will then will in you to perform that which you most desire. Show that hateful visitor the door and I will shut and bar it upon him; he will never reach as far as the citadel of your being; your spirit shall not be defiled.

Speaking with the utmost simplicity, I would say this means, "Do not fight the thing in detail: turn from it. Do not look at it at all, or at yourself, but only at your Lord." Satan was vanquished by Christ on the cross; he need never conquer us. There is full provision made for victory over all the power of the enemy. Take your victory then, and praise your Prince of Glory. Sing—"singing to yourselves" is a word of divine wisdom. Read—drive your thoughts into a new channel till they run there of themselves. Work—go and help lame dogs over stiles. Resolutely do something for someone else; and as you do this in dependence on Him who is the rightful Master of your house, the unwelcome visitor will vanish. The attempt of the evil one to destroy you will react upon himself, perhaps by weakening his grip on another soul, perhaps by furnishing you with the key to the confidence of one who needs your help—for all the deeper experiences of sorrow and comfort, temptation and victory, sooner or later turn into keys. You will not only conquer, you will be more than conqueror through Him who loved you.

Our Lord and Saviour Jesus Christ did not refuse dark woods: It became Him in bringing many sons unto glory, to make the Captain of their salvation perfect through sufferings. In all things it behooved Him to be made like unto His brethren. For in that He Himself hath suffered being tempted, He is able to succor them that are tempted. "All Christ's life was a cross and a martyrdom; and seekest thou to thyself rest and joy?" No, Lord, no. We will not seek these perishable treasures. I and the children whom Thou hast given me would come together to Thy Country, not one son or daughter missing. Therefore we pray Thee, help Thy servants, whom Thou hast redeemed with Thy precious blood, lest they flinch from the conditions of the way.

If our hearts be set on bringing many sons unto glory we cannot refuse what our Lord accepted; he who has not suffered being tempted cannot succor them that are tempted. But here the enemy comes at times with a knife in his hand and he thrusts it into the heart. Our holy Lord was never swept off His feet by some tremendous wave. To fall may cause another to fall. How can One who never fell, and so never caused anyone to fall, help a soul that is tempted to despair because of having hindered another? Our Saviour never suffered being tempted there. *How can He help me there?*

In searching for an answer to that question I have been led again to Calvary. The answer is found at the cross, and only at the cross. If one who loves can, by virtue of human love, plunge in spirit into gulfs unknown in actual experience to succor one beloved (and we know that love can do this), how much more can the divine? "He hath made Him to be sin for us who knew no sin": "Him who knew no sin He made to be sin on our behalf." Who has sounded the depths of that gulf? "And there was darkness over the whole land." There is no darkness where He cannot find us: if I make my bed in hell, behold, Thou art there.

4

The call to enter for the second time into any painful experience is a sign of our Lord's confidence. It offers a great opportunity. "The most powerful thing in your life is your opportunity," said Kleobulos of Lindos; it is also the most irretrievable. We must have clearness of vision and courage and a quiet mind if we are to see it, and lay hands upon it as it hurries past us on very quiet feet and disappears as utterly as the day that has gone: "As thy servant was busy here and there" it was gone. God give us vision and courage and a quiet mind.

Others have been in those woods. Their words, when they speak at all, are nearly always simple: "Whatsoever thou hearest, seest, or feelest, that should hinder thee in the way, abide not with it willfully, tarry not for it restfully, behold it not, like it not, dread it not; but ever go forth in thy way, and think thou wouldest be at Jerusalem. For *that* thou covetest, and *that* thou desirest, and naught else but that. And also if men would delay thee with tales and feed thee with falsehoods, to draw thee to mirths and to leave thy pilgrimage, make a deaf ear and answer not again, and say naught else but that thou wouldest be at Jerusalem. And if men proffer thee gifts and will make thee rich with worldly good, attend not to them; think ever on Jerusalem."

Yes, we would be at Jerusalem and at none other place but there. And as we journey, our heart fastened to this purpose so that none can shake us from it, our woods are enlightened to farthest rim.

We have called the wood dark because, as in the other wood, darkness must be crossed before the light is reached. But it is the light, not the darkness, that is remembered. The rough grass is like a bright carpet. The very substance of the tree trunk appears to be penetrated by light. We cannot see for the glory of that light. Dearly, very dearly, hast Thou loved us, O Jesus our Redeemer. Thou hast led us according to the integrity of Thy heart; and guided us by the skillfulness of Thy hands. Thou hast raised up Thy power and come among us; and with great might succored us. And in love has Thy word been fulfilled, "I will bring the blind by a way that they knew not; I will lead them in paths that they have not known: I will make darkness light before them, and crooked things straight. These things will I do unto them, and not forsake them."

But He could not forsake us: Can a woman forget, that she should not have compassion? Yea, they may forget, yet will I not forget thee. And we shall find that when we have to go again through some dark wood the angel of the Lord comes again the second time, and touches us, and says, "Arise and eat; because the journey is too great for thee"—kind angel, patient angel; he has a cruse of water ready and cake baked on the coals. For the angels are like their Lord: He had a fire of coals and fish laid thereon and bread ready for His tired fishermen. Hear Him in the storm: *"Be of good cheer; it is I; be not afraid."* And when they were afraid again: *"Why are ye troubled and why do thoughts arise in your hearts? It is I Myself."* Four words can be very consoling: *"It is I Myself."*

5

I suppose all of us know what it is to be comforted in this way; and we know what it is to want to share our comfort. A very dear comfort came to me recently after a day of some burden about one whose path just then led through the Second Wood.

This brought to mind the Second Storm.

When for the first time the disciples found themselves sorely tried by wind and raging water, their Master was with them in the boat; and it was only evening, not night, which made it much easier, even though He was asleep and even though the waves beat into the ship. The Second Storm was different. "It was now dark, and Jesus was not come to them."

"And only heaven is better than to walk with Christ at midnight over moonless seas," yes, *with Christ*—with Christ one's all but visible Companion. I think few of us would hesitate to go through anything if only we could see our Lord Jesus in the room with us, albeit asleep on a pillow. But the second test of faith is sharper than the first; the later must always be sharper than the earlier. This is the law of life. The story is a picture of life—as it feels, as it appears.

> A great wind blowing, raging sea,
> And rowers toiling wearily,
> Far from the land where they would be.

And then One coming, coming nearer every minute. They were still many furlongs distant from the land (so some manuscripts read). They were still toiling in rowing. Just when they needed Him most "they see Jesus walking on the sea and drawing nigh unto the ship."

> And then One coming, drawing nigh;
> They care not now for starless sky.
> The Light of Life says, "It is I."

> They care not now for toil of oar,
> For lo, the ship is at the shore,
> And their Beloved they adore.

> Lord of the Lake of Galilee,
> Who long ago walked on the sea,
> My heart is comforted in Thee.

The peace that is in this story sank softly into my heart that day, and afterwards I heard how "Jesus walking on the sea" had drawn nigh to him for whose sake I had been burdened. There was an operation which he had always dreaded (most of us have our private and peculiar dreads in such matters), and now he had heard that this particular operation was required. "And there wasn't the least dread. It had all gone," he said jubilantly. Quite evidently it had. And he told me of the word that had been given. "This also cometh forth from the Lord of hosts, which is wonderful in counsel and excellent in working." Was it not just like our Father to give that word? "He led them on safely, so that they feared not; *and they dreaded not,*" is Rotherham's rendering. Sometimes we would hardly admit to fear and yet we have a dread. God knows all about our dreads, and how to disperse them by a word of power and peace.

This little tale of today is told because so often we darken our woods by sadness over one dear to us whom we long to see relieved or released, and all the time the Lord of Light is shining on that heart, and speaking words that will never be forgotten, and which, handed on to others like a lighted torch, will travel, who can tell how far? We must learn to look on and see the far more exceeding and eternal weight of glory that is being prepared for our beloved.

Does St. Paul regret the thorn in the flesh that drew forth words that have comforted countless millions? Do the men for whom the winds were contrary wish they had been spared the storm that brought their Lord to them walking on the sea and caused Him to speak that immortal *It is I: be not afraid?* Could we wish to skirt a wood where our Master waited to give us a word to lighten the dark woods of others? No, not even now, while the pressure is upon us, would we choose, if we might, to escape from this which is but for a moment, and which worketh that which is eternal.

13

The Greenwood

1

AFTER the dark wood there is often a greenwood, and peaceful days that seem to breathe rest; and there is neither adversary nor evil occurrence. The quietness gives time for grateful thoughts about the way we have been led, such a wonderfully kind way. "Not one good thing hath failed of all the good things which He spoke concerning us; all are come to pass unto us, and not one thing hath failed thereof."[10] How often when we did not know what to do something happened for our help, and our feet were set in a large room.

It is good to give time to the greenwood. Quiet thoughts come there, and quiet prayers; for all about us speaks of quietness. And we too want to be quiet towards our God, like the low green moss, that vaunteth not itself.

> Like low green moss—and yet our thoughts are thronging;
>   Running to meet Thee, all alight, afire.
> Thirsty the soul that burneth in love-longing;
>   Fountain and fire art Thou, and heart's desire.
>
> Therefore, we come, Thy righteousness our cover,
>   Thy precious Blood our one, our only plea.
> Therefore we come, O Saviour, Master, Lover;
>   To whom, Lord, could we come save unto Thee?

But some have forgotten the way to that peaceful place. They have long ago been caught up in the whirl of machinery; there is a great restlessness, and they are much tossed about and perplexed. They see no plan, no pattern for their own life, or for mankind. Men groan from out of the city, and the soul of the wounded crieth out. A wounded spirit who can bear?

There are many ways out of that weary city: *And I said, This is my infirmity: but I will remember the years of the right hand of the Most High*. That *"I will remember"* reveals a byway from any street in the city into the heart of the greenwood. And if words fail us and even memory, we have this: "What can David say more unto Thee? for Thou, Lord God, knowest Thy servant." Just that simple *"Thou knowest Thy servant"* can reveal a way.

But to each is his own way. In a seacoast village in the north of Ireland I used to listen as a child to the fisher-folk and farmers singing,

> Goodness and mercy all my life
> > Shall surely follow me:
> And in God's house for evermore
> > My dwelling-place shall be.

The singing of that psalm, sung as it always was in the Scottish Metrical Version, seemed to open a sure byway out of the city into the greenwood.

Many an overwhelmed heart has found the way through carefully treasured letters of Samuel Rutherford: "Look to the east," he wrote, "the dawning of the glory is near. Your Guide is good company and knoweth all the miles, and the ups and downs. Ye cannot be marred, nor miscarry in His hand." And again, "Your faith may be boldly charitable of Christ, that however matters go, the worst shall be a tired traveler, and a joyful and sweet welcome home. The back of your winter night is broken. Look to the east; the day-sky is breaking. Think not that Christ loseth time or lingereth unsuitably. O fair, fair, and sweet morning." The writer of those letters was a tired traveler; he knew what it was to be pressured, but he has forgotten that now. And even in his traveling days he could forget. "No face looketh on me but it laugheth on me. I go soon to my King's palace at Aberdeen." And Aberdeen was his appointed prison.

I look at the leaves and grass and fern; no face looketh on me but it laugheth on me, the little sunlit leaves seem to laugh. They laugh with memories for me. For there was a day when for two of us no face looked on us but it laughed. A child who had been in danger of destruction had been given to us in open court after anxious months of spiritual fight, and she and I were returning home by a road running for miles under the mountains. We met and passed many people on that road. Some were in mat-covered bullock carts like our own; some were on foot. And we were so happy, the child and I, that we could not help leaning out of the open end of our cart and sending a smile to all our fellow wayfarers. And they smiled back at us. We were God's merry-men that day, and I always think of that road as the road of laughter and of smiles.

Such days are blessed gifts. They bless us, not only at the time, but a thousand times afterwards. There is no prison for the mind whose walls are bright with such pictures. The dreariest room is turned into my King's palace.

2

But some are fast in bonds, and to them the greenwood says softly—the words move in the mind like the whisper of wind among the trees—"Let not your heart be troubled, neither let it be afraid." It says, "The plant called heart's-ease often grows where we should not expect to find it." And it says, "After the sad days have passed you will look back and wonder how you were carried through. It will not always be so hard as it has been of late; for after darkness cometh light and after tempest cometh calm." And this is no fantasy. It shall be so.

Then our hearts go out to Him:

> O Lord beloved, my times are in Thy hand;
> My very minutes wait on Thy command.
> In this still room, O Blessed Master, walk
> And with my spirit talk.

It is in simple ways like this that the word is fulfilled: "In the multitude of my thoughts within me, Thy comforts delight my soul." The woodland picture may perhaps be one of the comforts, only a little one, but very little comforts can give pleasure, even as the very little globes of essence in the myrtle leaf can diffuse the fragrance of the myrtle. Thanks be to God for His little comforting things. And thank God too for the short and easy words in His Book. The least of us can understand them, the weariest can use them—words like the call of the bird when it hears some warning cry, "I flee unto Thee to hide me. Hide me under the shadow of Thy wings."

But life has been deepened by what we have gone through since first we turned sharply into the dark wood, and if we are in some greenwood now, we are instinctively on the alert lest we be caught in the meshes of any net of luxury. "For he that spends his time in sports, and calls it recreation, is like him whose garment is all made of fringes and his meat nothing but sauce." One of our Fellowship away on holiday writes of his dread of the fringes and sauce: "There is such a loving thought and care here that I sometimes fear lest the soldier-spirit may be weakened rather than strengthened. Everything is made so easy and so comfortable that I feel more than ever the need of the inner, private discipline which defends the soul against sloth and slackness."

From subtle love of softening things,
From easy choices, weakenings
(Not thus are spirits fortified,
Not this way went the Crucified),
From all that dims Thy Calvary,
O Lamb of God, deliver me.

We cannot be held fast in peace and nerved to inner, private discipline—to a soldiership that knows nothing of reserve to love that can plunge into very hell to save a soul, unstained by the foulness, unshriveled by the heat—unless we live within sight of Calvary. God forgive us for the strange coldness of so much of our love. The calculating love of Christians is the shame of the Church and the astonishment of angels. By Thine agony and bloody sweat; by Thy cross and passion; by Thy precious death and burial; by Thy glorious resurrection and ascension; and by the coming of the Holy Ghost, from the sin of coldness, Good Lord, deliver us.

3

It is His intention to deliver us from the coldness of a wandering love. When perilous influences try to draw us from the only life that is worth living there is resistance something like that which Southerns describes in his *Electricity and the Structure of Matter.*

If a plate of copper be held in the hands between the poles of a powerful electromagnet, all is quiet. But if it be "suddenly snatched away from the magnet, a considerable resistance is felt, as though some invisible agency were trying to prevent its motion—which indeed is the case. If one could see the electrons in the plate while it is being moved rapidly through the strong magnetic field which exists between the poles, they would be found to be circulating energetically in closed curves within the metal, and continually bombarding the atoms of the metal."

In the poles of the powerful magnet I see the powers of the love of God; in the field of magnetic force, the sphere of that love; in the copper plate, the lover who would fain abide there. (Hold Thou me up and I shall be safe.) And should another try to interfere and snatch him away from that place of his choice, something within him instantly resists, "as though some invisible agency" were set upon preventing his withdrawal.

For so, in very truth, the Spirit within him strives, that blessed Spirit of whom it is written that He yearneth over us. Who does not know the agitation, the turmoil of the soul that is in danger of leaving the place of its rest? Not easily do we drift from our home in the love of God. And this brings us to our knees. "O Thou Good Omnipotent, who so carest for every one of us as if Thou caredst for him only; and so for all, as if they were but one; let me know Thee, O Lord, who knowest me: let me know Thee as I am known. Power of my soul, enter into it, and fit it for Thee, *that Thou mayest have and hold it without spot or wrinkle.*"

There is a way into the greenwood which is not much used in these days of feverish rush. Its name in the Scriptures is Meditation. ("Let my meditation be sweet unto Him.") We would plow a deeper furrow if we knew more of that way. We would be quieter then, and there is nothing creative in noise. "Friend, when dost thou think?" asked an old Quaker after seeing a student's class schedule. We cannot think by acting like machinery. We cannot consider the lilies without giving time to the lilies. Often our flash of haste means little. To read a book in an hour (if the book has taken half a lifetime to write) means nothing at all. To pray in a hurry of spirit means nothing. To live in a hurry means to do much but effect little. We build more quickly in wood, hay, and stubble than in gold, silver, precious stones; but the one abides, the other does not.

If he who feels the world is too much with him will make for himself a little space, and let his mind settle like a bee in a flower on some great word of his God, and brood over it, pondering it till it has time to work in him, he will find himself in the greenwood.

He will meet his Lord there, and then quite certainly he will soon be looking with his Lord's eyes upon the world. He will see it as Nehemiah saw the city wall, broken down, its gates burned with fire. He will hear great words of commission: "So shalt thou be called a Repairer of broken walls, a Restorer of paths leading home."[11] He will gather others around him: "Come, let us build up the walls." He will find something that fits his mood in the brave story: "So we labored in the work: and half of them held the spears from the rising of the morning till the stars appeared." And as he reads he will be all a prayer:

Make me Thy laborer.
Let me not dream of ever looking back;
Let not my knees be feeble, hands be slack;
O make me strong to labor, strong to bear,
From the rising of the morning until the stars appear.

Make me Thy warrior,
On whom Thou canst depend to stand the brunt
Of any perilous charge on any front;
Give to me skill to handle sword and spear,
From the rising of the morning until the stars appear.

Not far from us, those stars—
Unseen as angels, and yet looking through
The quiet air, the day's transparent blue.
What shall we know, and feel, and see, and hear
When the sunset colors kindle and evening stars appear?

4

This writing and the life of the day are closely intertwined. That prayer-song was written down, and then the mail brought

letters from many countries. Some were Rose-letters, as we call
those that come from thorny places like hospitals and yet tell of
comforting roses. They often make me want to revise the little
Rose From Brier book, for its writer barely knows the alphabet
of pain, and its readers know so much more than that. One told
of how the patient "all bandaged up could at last read with part
of an eye," and another told of a captive to a "dreadful kind of
bone disease" who in that far land of great distress was finding
the flowers of God. And because I know that to some like these
such a prayer as "Make me Thy laborer, Make me Thy warrior,"
may be almost a hurt, I will add something with them, and only
them, in mind.

The hardest laboring and fighting is not that which
engages hands and feet and busy brain. It is done out of sight.
In those secret places where Spirit deals with spirit, and spirit
yields itself up to Spirit, forces are at work whose powers we
have no means of measuring. The doctor, the nurse, the ward
maid, the visitor, see only an ordinary bed, and the one in
that bed feels like a worm and no man many a time, but the
Unseen Watchers see a powerhouse. Travelers set forth from
that bed and they reach the uttermost corners of the earth.
Long prayer is not needed to send them forth. "Short prayer
pierceth heaven." A word, a look is enough. This labor and this
fighting can go on, and will (if the spirit be kept in tune with
the Eternal Spirit), from the rising of the morning till the stars
appear. This is life at its hardest. For I do not think that there
is any comparison between the hardness of such a life and life
in the open, when we labored in the work with our sword
girded by our side, and he that sounded the trumpet was not
far off—there is something exhilarating in the sound of the
trumpet, and it is delightful to build the wall in company
with willing fellow builders. But what if He who has kept the
hardest until now has kept also His good wine until now? It
would be just like Him to do that.

In the mountain forests to the west of Dohnavur our children find the cocoon of the atlas moth. It hangs from a twig, like a small brown bag tied up and left there and forgotten, a mere two inches of papery bag, and however often we see it we are never prepared for the miracle that emerges. For miracle it is: a large, almost birdlike creature struggles slowly through the very narrow neck of the bag. It has wings of crimson and pink, and blended green of various soft tones, shading off into terracotta, brown, old-gold. Each wing has a window made of a clear substance like a delicate flake of talc, and on the edge of each is a pattern of wavy lines or dots, or some other dainty device. From wingtip to wingtip, nine, sometimes ten, inches of beauty, one of God's lovely wonders—that is what comes out of the brown paper bag. Nothing preserved in a glass case can show it, for the colors fade, but fresh from the hands of its Creator it is like something seen in a dream, pure fairyland.

The radiant emergence of butterfly from chrysalis has often been used to illustrate that which will be when we put on immortality, but I am thinking of this exquisite thing in another way now. What if our life within these detaining months or years be like the life within the dull brown bag of the cocoon? One day something will emerge to the glory of His grace. Can we not, then, sustained by the Bread of heaven and the Good Wine, continue in this hidden labor and spiritual fight till the sunset colors kindle and the stars appear?

14

Gold Leaf and Lilies

1

IF only we are content to go on laboring, warring, trusting, faithful in a very little, we are led by humble, quiet ways into the will of God, that will which has willed our good from our earliest days until now.

Our nursery thinking lies at the back of our grown-up thought. Gold leaf and lily buds have always made me think of the plans of God, because as a small child I was given a book with gold leaf, and about the same time heard someone quote, "God's plans like lilies, pure and white, unfold," and learned to wait for the opening of the close-shut green buds of the lilies in the garden; learned, too, to listen:

> He in our childhood with us walks,
> And with our thoughts mysteriously He talks;
> He often visiteth our minds.

There came a day when I saw golden lilies. It was in a wood in Japan. There was a wall of sheer blue mountain, like the mountain in the greenwood picture; blue sky was showing through the leaves, and everywhere in sheets of flame and gold there were lilies. The old thoughts of childhood met me in that wood, and I was back in my nursery, carefully holding the "book of gold" in my hands.

That book was a tiny thing, but it was magical to me. Its pages were of paper of a curious quality, pinkish in color, fine, firm and untearable. Between them lay the flakes of gold leaf, so delicate that a breath would blow them away, and yet if you were very gentle you could lift them up without crumpling them. They were enchantment, a charm that never wore thin; and anything partly made of wonder (like the opening of a lily bud) and partly of brightness (like the shining of gold leaf) became for me a synonym for the plans of God: so that when I lately read of how gold, that closely compacted metal, becomes transparent ("pure gold like unto clear glass"), it was like seeing a light fall on something that had long lain in a dim corner of one's room.

For the plans of God for our lives, laid one on the other like the cubic crystals of gold that make up the texture of gold leaf, do often become clear as we go on. We look, and are astonished as we see how all the way by which He has led us, every lesson He has caused us to learn, all the spiritual discipline of the years, converge upon a single point, now at last perceived. We understand, in part at least, why He has led us so. His golden thoughts of love toward us, slowly unfolding in His providence, are transparent now, pure gold, as it were transparent glass.

But there is one question gold does not answer. "Why it should be green when looked through is a mystery."[12] The X-ray has told why, when it is beaten out to about the 150,000th part of an inch in thickness, it permits the transmission of the rays of light; but why only green rays? Why should the other colors of the spectrum be absorbed, and green alone be transmitted? We do not know. But as in such earthly matters questions unanswered today are answered tomorrow, so it is in the things of the heavenlies. Then shall we know even as also we are known.

2

The memory of the nursery and its book of gold (the

technical name for such a book) passes in the glimmering way of such memories into thoughts of another room and another book. The room is very quiet, for the father of the family lies there dying, but the children do not know that yet. They only know that he is ill, and when he asks his eldest child to read to him she finds her way to Samson Agonistes, and to this:

> All is best, though we oft doubt,
>   What th' unsearchable dispose
> Of highest wisdom brings about,
>   And ever best found in the close.

And here the reading ended, without a thought that it was the last time father and child would read together, or that the next words to be specially associated with that room would be words of consolation from the God of the widow, *"The Lord is good, a stronghold in the day of trouble; and He knoweth them that trust in Him."*

But Scripture and poem are one with lily bud and the gold leaf in their reticence. The unsearchable operation of Wisdom is still an untracked field, and we are not told why there must be such a day of trouble that if the Lord were not our stronghold we would be overwhelmed.

Sometimes even in reputable writing a strange ignorance speaks up, objecting. A hymn for protection on the sea is sung; the ship of which the singers were thinking is lost at sea. A railway journey is the subject of prayer; the train is derailed—and so on through a crowd of calamities. "How do you account for it?"

We do not attempt to account for it. We only know the outskirts of His ways; and how small a whisper do we hear from Him. As well try to capture the motif of a symphony from a few bars imperfectly heard, or imagine the finished picture after seeing the colors on the palette, or master the argument of the book of Job after reading a few paragraphs, as presume to imagine that we who see only a fragment of the thought of God can understand the whole or interpret it to another. But we shall not be disappointed when we are told the secret of the mysteries of this present. The word stands true: "And ever best found in the close."

The enemy will contest our confidence at every point; he will remind us of the human cause of our trouble. But faith looks above the human. "They sold Joseph to the Ishmaelites for twenty pieces of silver: and they brought Joseph into Egypt. . . . I am Joseph your brother, whom ye sold into Egypt. . . . *God did send me before you* to preserve life for you; ye thought evil against me, *but God meant it unto good. . . . He sent a man before them, even Joseph.*"

If our thoughts linger among the brothers and the Ishmaelites we shall miss the precious things that were the portion of Joseph. We shall never be a fruitful bough, even a fruitful bough by a well, whose branches run over the wall, blessing all who seek them with their shade and fruit. We shall wither like the plants in the desert where no water is. Desperate things can happen—things that are in every way wrong—but faith overlooks the earthly. Faith sees God. Faith can even console those who were the human instruments of the hurt: "Now therefore be not grieved nor angry with yourselves that ye sold me hither. . . . Fear not, I will nourish you and your little ones. And he comforted them and spoke kindly unto them." Faith worketh by love.

In the earlier years of the work in Dohnavur we were constantly reminded of how there came a messenger unto Job and said. . . . And while he was yet speaking there came also another, and said . . .—for trouble followed trouble very much after the fashion of those messengers.

One evening, in a brief lull between the messengers, two of us spent an hour with a small telescope looking at the Great Nebula in Orion. As I looked into those deeps of darkness lighted by an infinitely far and faint pale flame, a sense of the eternal came upon me. *The world passeth away and the lust thereof, and the grief thereof, and the wrong thereof, but he that doeth the will of God abideth forever,* was the word of that breath of flame. The transitory appeared (as we know it to be) in comparison with the eternal of no account at all. I knew then that the only thing that matters when trouble is appointed is our attitude towards that trouble; and I turned from the telescope to meet the next assault with an entirely new peace. This that I must touch and handle and feel was nothing of real moment. A few days or months or years, and it would be forgotten utterly. But how I touched and handled it, how I felt and acted towards those who caused it— that belonged to the eternal order. It belonged to the things that would abide when earth and the heavens shall wax old as doth a garment, and as a vesture shall be folded up.

3

In every spiritual work for God there is need for one, several, or many (according to the size of the work) to be continually on the alert to detect the approach of the enemy of souls. For where there is no vision the people perish, the work languishes, prayer runs thin. A favorite wile of that enemy is to create a preoccupation with the messengers, the brothers, the Ishmaelites. But the watcher is not deceived; he looks past the servants and sees their master. ("Is not the hand of Joab with thee in all this?") Then, for he has boldness to enter the holiest by the blood of Jesus, he meets his foe and his Lord's foe there. In no other place can that foe be met and foiled and his sting drawn out. His devices may appear to succeed, but they are powerless to injure, and in the end his attack fails miserably.

The watcher learns many things as he is taught to watch. He learns never to be tired of loving, never to be shocked or startled out of his peace in Christ, never to be astonished by anything the devil does, never for one moment to forget that though he may be baffled his Captain is not and never can be. Every high thing was cast down at Calvary. Principalities and powers were spoiled there. He made a show of them openly, triumphing over them. We have to do with a conquered, not a conquering, foe; we follow a Captain who is unconquerable.

When the worker for God is in heaviness because of the souls committed to his care, when he travails in spirit and does not see the fruit of his travail, when he sees no way to deal with some deadly thing that has sprung to life in their midst, he has peace even in the moment of keenest anxiety in remembering the sovereignty of his Lord. And if he has to take action and knows not what to do, the words *He that is perfect in knowledge is with thee*, trusted to the full, will be like the Lord's "Peace, be still" to the winds and the waves. There will be a great calm. If something must be done immediately then a way will be shown. If it be possible to wait there will be peace until clearness comes, and when it is given there will be strength to act.

And so we return to Milton and his unshakable confidence. The vast design of Providence is design, not accident. Brothers, Ishmaelites, messengers, the doings of the opposing powers, however ably directed by a master hand, all have their place in that design. The secret things belong unto the Lord, *"and ever best found in the close."*

4

This truth is a lighted stronghold. We must dwell therein or perish. Without the light that streams from the windows of that tower the history of mankind is one long, dark confusion, an almost unbroken riot of evil and callous cruelty. God has always had His little sanctuaries; homes of tranquility and even sometimes "choirs and places where they sing"; but everywhere life shows a tortured face. Everywhere we see chaos, feel suffering, and hear the cry of questions. All literature echoes those questions:

> O Zeus, for our lords is there
> > Naught but despair?
> No path through the tangle of evils, no loosing
> > Of chains that have bound them?

"Now gods that we adore, whereof comes this?" "Do you see this, O God?" "When didst Thou sleep when such a deed was done?" "Lord, how long wilt Thou look upon this?" "Are there demons among men, clothed with humanity?" Strip the veneer and illusion from our own age and what do we see? A chasm opens at our feet and we cannot cross it. . . .

"I write unto you, little children, because ye have known the Father." To know our Father is to know that He is in charge of the universe. "I bear up the pillars of it, I uphold the order of the world, I, not you, My burdened child. All souls are Mine"—that is His word to us in the hours of our oppression.

There must have been such hours for all thinkers from the earliest ages onwards. But men were not left to grope in bewilderment. Night unto night showeth knowledge. Before the sure word of prophecy shone like a light that shineth in a dark place, the seers of God saw in the skies the signs and tokens of His purpose and providence. When our Lord Jesus Christ stooped down and wrote on the floor of this dusty earth no man read what He wrote there, and the wind soon blew the dust away. But when He wrote in the skies that starry dust was not blown away, nor were the great words hidden from man. Tradition has it that Enoch read the writing of the stars. Perhaps God taught it to him when he walked with Him. When we study that writing (the signs of the Zodiac and their decans) we find that all around the circle, from Virgo to Leo, close by every symbol of evil there is a symbol of good. And the good is always shown as conquering the bad: "For this, for this the lights innumerable as symbols shine."

So we come back to rest: There may be darkness about our ways as there has always been and still is about the ways of the world. There are times when neither sun nor stars in many days appear, and no small tempest lies on us and all hope that we shall be saved is taken away, and yet—blessed paradox—we are never left without that which the old Scottish minister likened to moonlight. ("It is possible to gather gold, where it may be had, with moonlight.")

There comes a liturgy,
Even for a little span,
Great voices Christian,
Songs of my Lord to me,
To me, a simple man.

The sea-wave crashes in my ears:
Again their viols cease:
I have been here for endless years,
And the room is full of peace.

Dim-sliding harmonies
And dreaming voice of seers
Come past all barriers.
With God I have no fears,
And round me roll His seas,

sang God's fool, the Mystic, in his hour of exultation. Not dreaming voices only, but strong vibrant voices, the voices of the gallant, the crusaders of the spiritual world who have preferred Jerusalem above their chief joy; and His hidden ones, God's violets among souls—they come too. No barriers can forbid them. And when they come the room is full of peace.

This for today; what of tomorrow? We have no doubt about

tomorrow: there is always something in the thought of our Father that is more profound and more beautiful than anything that we can imagine. Who has seen, who has described the lilies that grow in His Garden of Tomorrow? Not even the angels of God, who from time to time have told so much to man, have ever told him anything about those lilies.

15

The Wall with a Window

1

THEREFORE, child of the Father, let not your heart be troubled. The words have still their ancient power to calm the soul of man. And after we have listened a while we go about our common business with a new courage, and as we give our whole mind to the duty of the hour He comes sometimes privily, when we are least aware of Him. "But thou shalt full well know Him ere He go; for wonderfully He stirreth and mightily turneth thine heart into beholding of His goodness, and doth melt thine heart delectably, as wax against the fire, into softness of His love. But then He goeth ere thou wit it. For He withdraweth Himself somewhat, not in all, but from excess into sobriety; the highness passeth, but the substance and the effect of grace dwelleth still."

But then He goeth ere thou wit it. Not that He has left us, for that can never be, but that for love-reasons He has withdrawn something that was ours before, and which we miss. And though the substance and effect still remain, we feel as one might who, after large freedom, was pent between walls. It is a familiar trial. It is the dryness that we touched upon before. But there is a window in the wall (there is no wall without a window); through patience and through comfort of the Scriptures we have hope, and that hope maketh not ashamed. It is the virtue of our Lord's word relied upon, apart from any feeling, that opens a way of deliverance.

And it is the loving witness to Him that recovers our departed happiness. "What is thy Beloved more than another Beloved?" the daughters of Jerusalem ask the bride, who, just then, does not know where her Beloved is. But she tells them what she can of His beauty. And when they asked her, "Whither is thy Beloved gone that we may seek Him with thee?" she can tell them where He is, for now at last she knows: "My Beloved is gone down into His garden."

2

There is a wall that can rise around one who has drifted from his Lord. It is built up by an irreverent habit of mind. A familiar, casual naming of the Name that is above every name must grieve the Holy Spirit, of whom it is written, "He shall glorify Me." The grieved Spirit always withdraws from the soul that is careless about grieving Him, and He will not return till that soul is on its knees. Till then it will be within walls and it will find no window.

Or the wall may be solid all around us because of our neglect of the Scriptures, and by much dealing in books "limed with the mixture of the syllables" of His name like the talk of certain men of whom St. Augustine wrote. He wrote also of the books that he had read in his search for truth, many and huge books: "And these were the dishes wherein to me, hungering after Thee, they, instead of Thee, served up the Sun and Moon, beautiful works of Thine, but yet Thy works, not Thyself."

Those dishes, glittering fantasies "which by our eyes deceive our mind," were set before him, much as they are set before us now. He might indeed be writing of some of our books, which offer us only "beautiful works," not the Lord of Life Himself. "Yet because I thought them to be Thee, I fed thereon; not eagerly, for Thou didst not in them taste to me as Thou art; for Thou wast not these emptinesses, nor was I nourished by them, but exhausted rather. Food in sleep shows very like our food awake; yet those asleep are not nourished by it, for they are asleep. But those were not even any way like to Thee, as Thou hast now spoken to me." Many a disenchanted reader has echoed those words: Those books are not even any way like to Thee, as Thou hast now spoken to me, O Jesus, Lover of souls.

And so there are walls of doubt and of distress of mind that need not be. To lose one's spiritual liberty is a deadly thing. To stay within those walls is death. *"Never let what you know be disturbed by what you do not know."* "You have eaten too much of the tree of knowledge" (often falsely so called); "eat more of the tree of life," said an old minister to a younger one who had lost his first love.

Turn from the glittering fantasies and the lure of smooth language. Read that Book the sum of whose words is Truth. Lord, to whom shall we go? Thou hast the words of eternal life. Those words will open a window that no blast of hell can shut; we shall fly like a bird through our window then; our soul will know the freedom of the woods. But we need to be very simple and humble if we are to find that window.

3

Human distress of any kind can build walls. So can circumstances which, however they may appear to others, are painful to the one concerned. The wall may be like this ivied wall, or it may be as bare as a slab of cement. Beauty or bareness makes no difference. If we see no door anywhere, or if the doors be all barred and bolted even though the fair wide heaven be above, the place within that wall is prison to us—until we see our window.

And when we see it we are free; for in the spiritual world to see out is to be out. We are where our thoughts are, just as we are where our love is. "For where your treasure is, there will your heart be also."

Bewilderment can wall us in: "I have seen the wicked in great power and spreading himself like a green bay tree." We see such men flourish: they are not in trouble as other men; neither are they plagued like other men. This, as we all know, is continually and literally true. The tabernacles of robbers prosper, and they that provoke God are secure. "They hatch cockatrice' eggs, and weave the spider's web: he that eateth of their eggs dieth, and that which is crushed breaketh out into a viper." We have seen the innocent stung by the vipers that crawl out of those eggs: "Then was my heart grieved." And a grieved heart is walled.

But there is a swift way of escape: "When I thought to know this"—the mystery of apparently triumphant iniquity—"it was too painful for me; until I went into the sanctuary of God." And after a little while spent in that quiet place we find our peace in prayer: "O let the wickedness of the ungodly come to an end. Fill their faces with shame, that they may seek Thy name, O Lord. Thy kingdom come. Thy will be done on earth as it is in heaven."

Sometimes we pile up the stones ourselves. We take some promise in our Book, isolate it, forget other scriptures that may bear upon it; interpret it, perhaps unconsciously, according to our own desire, and then stake our all upon it. "Call upon Me in the day of trouble: I will deliver thee and thou shalt glorify Me." I will deliver thee from the day of trouble? Thank God, it may be so. A spiritual airplane may swoop down and carry the assaulted one far out of reach of his foe. But sometimes he sees no wings in the sky; only the Shepherd draws very near, and a soft little song fills the valley: "Yea, though I walk through the valley of the shadow of death, I will fear no evil; for Thou art with me; Thy rod and Thy staff they comfort me."

To see an alternative meaning in a promise may open a window, and to see such a window open after a shadowy day is like seeing a moonflower open in the dusk. All day long it has kept its bud folded close, a long, twisted, pointed tube. But now it slowly unfurls till it is a wide-open bell. And deep within it always lies a little coronet of diamonds, a dew of light.

4

Healing in illness by the Touch of God, as apart from His use of His own gifts of help, is unforgettable. To know that indeed the power of the Spirit has quickened our mortal body to run and not be weary, to walk and not faint, long after the natural power has broken and gone, is a deep and solemn joy.

But is one who has proved the Healer in this way asked to be satisfied with something different, something that appears at first sight to himself and to others to be less to the glory of God than healing by the Touch would be? If that child of the Father be dwelling deep in the Father's love, too deep to be disturbed by any noise of words, then all is well. But if he has wandered from his rest then there will be something like that earlier picture in the Song of Songs: "The voice of my Beloved! Behold, He standeth behind our wall, He looketh in at the windows, He showeth Himself through the lattice."

The Beloved is never content to be "behind our wall," on the other side, as it were. He looketh in at the windows. The Lord turned and looked upon Peter. He turns that same melting look of love upon the one who has allowed a wall to grow up between himself and his Beloved. And with that look will come to mind the word of a more faithful lover: "I am filling up as required what is lacking in the afflictions of our Christ, in my flesh, on behalf of His body, which is the Church."

The words seem too great and heavenly to be approached by anything so small and earthly as we are, and I know too little of their meaning to do more than quote them from the translation in Moule's *Colossian Studies*, where he adds this note: "He (Paul) is thinking not of our Lord's *passion*, but of His sacred *Life-*

work. (He only *began* to do and to teach.) Every true soldier and sufferer for Him and His flock contributes to the filling up of that incompleteness, so far as he toils and bears in Christ." And Elliot helps by his translation of "afflictions": *hard and galling pressure.* Bonds can be that. But what do they matter if only we may suffer in behalf of the glory of God?

5

The bountiful supply of all our needs according to His riches in glory in Christ Jesus is one of the things that are of good report—things that are sweet to speak of, as the word has been translated. Many a servant of the Master occupied in His business has seen tables spread in the wilderness and has told of his tables to the praise of the mercy of God. But if there be no miracles of ravens and brooks, meal in a barrel, oil in a cruse? Then he is called into a new fellowship: "Even unto this present hour we both hunger, and thirst, and are naked, and are buffeted, and have no certain dwelling-place; and labor, working with our own hands; being reviled, we bless; being persecuted, we suffer it; being defamed, we entreat: we are made as the filth of the world, and are the offscouring of all things unto this day."

When this happens we may miss an opportunity, which perhaps angels covet, to speak good of His name. If we pity ourselves we shall be far from Him who refused the soft "pity thyself" of human affection. If we accept the kind of sympathy which says in effect about anything He allows to be, "This is hard," we shall be like the servant who so little knew his master that he could say to him, "I knew thee that thou art an hard man." In our hearts we know that all is well: we have a treasure in the heavens that faileth not, where no thief approacheth, neither moth corrupteth; but others cannot see our hearts. If Christians are the only Bible that the world reads, what manner of persons ought they to be?

"I said, I will keep my mouth with a bridle."

But it is not enough to be silent and to hold my peace even from good because of those who observe me and do not understand the doings of my Lord. I must go further than that. So, as with heavenly intent, next to the psalm of the bridle or muzzle is the psalm of the New Song, even praise unto our God; many shall see it and fear (for the songs of the Lord are not only heard with the ear but seen by the eyes) and shall trust in the Lord.

Before a song can be put in the mouth it must be "learned by heart." There are times when the music of heaven appears to overflow to the earth, and we understand the words written about the worship in the Friends' Meeting House, when the silence was not dead but vital:

> Oh then call not silent,
>   Hours so full of singing.
> Even now, from wall to wall,
>   Hear the echoes ringing.

There are times when we hear nothing. And yet if we are quiet we shall presently hear. And having heard we shall sing. And it may be that when we look back from the Celestial Country, where there are no walls but the jeweled walls of the City whose gates shall not be shut at all, we shall know that the songs that echo longest are those we first heard and then learned to sing in the days when we seemed walled in, and then found our window.

6

We all have our special windows in the wall. Over one the word Dothan is written. It may look out upon Psalm 34:7: "The angel of the Lord encampeth round about them that fear Him, and delivereth them." That is Elisha's Dothan—the Dothan of

relief, protection, angelic interposition. Or it may be Joseph's—
"We saw the anguish of his soul," that was the memory burnt
upon his brothers' minds, for that was what Dothan had meant
to Joseph. And God knew it.

But He did not fill the mountain with shining companies
for the succor of that anguished soul. He seemed to do nothing.
And Joseph saw nothing, heard nothing. But perhaps he heard
more than we are told. *Is it not lawful for Me to do what I will with
Mine own? And blessed is he whosoever shall not be offended in Me.*
Such words belong to the Dothan of Joseph. They have power
to nerve to long endurance. Little human words of consolation
patter like raindrops on a roof. They cannot do much to reinforce
the inward man in times of real stress. They are like ineffectual
fireflies. As the Tamils would say: "Will darkness retire before the
light of fireflies?" But the word of Him who is Light enlightens
the eyes. The Lord my God will enlighten my darkness—any
darkness.

And so we will not fear to follow Him though He may lead
through the Dothan of Joseph and not of Elisha:

> I follow where Thou leadest; what are bruises?
> There are cool leaves of healing on Thy tree;
> Lead Thou me on. Thy heavenly wisdom chooses
>   In love for me.
>
> Thy lover then, like happy homing swallow
> That crosses hill and plain and lonely sea,
> All unafraid, so I will fearless follow,
>   For love of Thee.

It is all very simple, but it goes deep. And it leads to our Lord
and Redeemer. He knew what it was to be "inclosed" for our
sake. In that dark hour His window looked out upon another
view than this that we see through the window in the wall. He
did not see a sunny garden and a shady wood climbing a hillside.
His garden was Gethsemane; His hill was Calvary. But He saw

beyond that garden and that hill—"Who, for the joy that was set before Him, endured the cross, despising the shame, and is set down at the right hand of the throne of God."

The shadows of the underworld
    Compassed about my guilty soul;
And thunderbolts were on me hurled,
    And lightnings flashed. And on a scroll
Was written down, without, within,
The secret of my hidden sin.

Without, within, I saw it stand,
    In clearest words accusing me,
Till, as it were, a wounded hand
    Annulled its record, set me free.
With that the stormy wind did cease.
A voice commanded: there was peace.

O Saviour, stricken for my sin,
    O God, who gayest Him to grief,
O Spirit, who didst woo and win
    My troubled soul to seek relief,
O Love revealed at Calvary,
Thy glory lights eternity!

16

Go to Him and See

THESE chapters have been written to fellow lovers, but perhaps one who does not know our Saviour well enough to love Him will read this page. May the Lover of us all turn it to a signpost showing clearly the way Home.

There can be nothing more sorrowful than not to know the way, or having known it to have lost it.

In the cathedral of Lubeck, in Germany, there is an old inscription:

Ye call Me Master, and obey Me not.
Ye call Me Light, and see Me not.
Ye call Me Way, and take Me not.
Ye call Me Life, and desire Me not.
Ye call Me Wise, and follow Me not.
Ye call Me Fair, and love Me not.
Ye call Me Rich, and ask Me not.
Ye call Me Eternal, and seek Me not.
Ye call Me Gracious, and trust Me not.
Ye call Me Noble, and serve Me not.
Ye call me Mighty, and honor Me not.
If I condemn you, blame Me not.

But it is far from our Lord's desire to condemn us. "I became thoroughly miserable while a thorn was fastened in me" is the Septuagint rendering of Psalm 32:4. He wore a crown of thorns

that the thorn of unforgiven sin might be plucked out of my
heart. Hear what comfortable words our Saviour Christ saith
unto all that truly turn to Him: *Come unto Me, all that travail
and are heavy laden, and I will refresh you.*

To the hurt, the puzzled, the troubled, the sinful, I would
repeat what Faithful said to Hopeful when he thought that his
Saviour was not willing to receive him: "He bade me go to Him
and see." There is no doubt what will happen then: it has always
happened. To the pilgrim at the wicket gate, "'I am willing with
all My heart,' said He, and with that He opened the gate."

2

In the days of the Mutiny in India there was a young officer
in the Royal Fusiliers who was seeking for light. He had tried the
"glittering fantasies" but had found nothing there. "The more
I read, the more weary I got. What were they? Fiction. What I
wanted was fact, truth; yea, eternal truth. At last I threw them
all away, and stuck more and more to my Bible. At length the
light burst on my soul.

"I was riding back from mess one night upon my camel,
grieving over the uselessness of my life for the glory of God and
the good of man, when, as a ray from heaven, there came into
my mind the verse, 'All we like sheep have gone astray; we have
turned every one to his own way; and the Lord hath laid on Him
the iniquity of us all.' The iniquity of us all? Then all *my* iniquity—
that means, all my sins of omission as well as commission—all
laid by God on Christ, all borne away, all forgiven. Oh, the joy!
Oh, the peace! I got down from my camel, ran to my room,
and falling on my knees before God, praised and blessed Him
and the Lord Jesus Christ. I have often since been grieved and
distressed by sin, but I have, thank God, never, never lost that
peace, the peace of free, full, and eternal forgiveness of sins
through the blood of Christ."

It was enough. Conscience and heart were at rest at last. And now as he says simply, "I was helped by being a soldier, for I had begun to read my Bible as I read the Queen's Regulations, as if all its instructions were intended to be followed out."

Those rays from heaven are continually falling, but God, who never makes two flowers alike, or even two leaves or two blades of grass, never repeats Himself in the history of souls; and this conversion on camelback does, I think, stand out with a delightful unusualness. I have chosen a tale of years ago rather than one more recent because it need not break off abruptly as a recent story must, leaving a question in the mind about the race still to be run. That young officer (Major Malan—the name looks back to the martyrs of Merindol) ran a straight race through good report and ill. His was the loving spirit that set many another on fire.

3

Our confidence is not rooted in anything of ourselves—our seeing, hearing, feeling. The roots of an assurance which will stand the shocks of life and the solemn hour of death run deep into the word of the living God, so that if tonight "without a screen in one burst be seen the Presence in which I have ever been," I may have confidence.

"The Spirit of the Lord is upon Me, because He hath anointed Me to preach the gospel to the poor, He hath sent Me to heal the broken-hearted, to preach deliverance to the captives, and recovering of sight to the blind—*to strengthen with forgiveness those that are bruised*," so the Aramaic ends that word of peace.

"Come unto Me. Him that cometh unto Me I will in no wise cast out. If we confess our sins, He is faithful and just to forgive us our sins, and to cleanse us from all unrighteousness. The blood of Jesus Christ His Son cleanseth us from all sin." And (for without this truth we have only half a gospel) He is "able to keep you from falling, and to present you faultless before the presence of His glory with exceeding joy"—here is sure ground for faith.

There was one who was troubled because the Lord Jesus, to whom she did desire truly to come, seemed a long way off. And then in His mercy He stooped to speak with her:

> Below, above, around thee everywhere—
> So is My love, like clearness of blue air.
>
> To find the air so high and yet so low,
> Tell Me, beloved, hast thou far to go?
>
> •   •   •
>
> So high, so low—but I had thought Thee far,
> Remote, aloof, like glory of a star.
>
> And is the way of love so near to me?
> Then by that way I come; I come to Thee.

"For to Him who is everywhere, men come not by traveling but by loving." St. Augustine's beautiful words are seeds of light; I sow them on the page in faith that they will spring up as seeds do, thou knowest not how, perhaps for a Mary: "Jesus saith unto her, Mary. She turned herself, and saith unto Him, Rabboni; which is to say, Master." Perhaps for a Thomas: "Then saith He to Thomas, Reach hither thy finger, and behold My hands; and reach hither thy hand, and thrust it into My side: and be not faithless but believing. And Thomas answered and said unto Him, My Lord and my God."

> And is the way of love so near to me?
> Then by that way I come; I come to Thee.

"For to Him who is everywhere, men come not by traveling but by loving." St. Augustine's beautiful words are seeds of light; I sow them on the page in faith that they will spring up as seeds do, thou knowest not how, perhaps for a Mary: "Jesus saith unto her, Mary. She turned herself, and saith unto Him, Rabboni; which is to say, Master." Perhaps for a Thomas: "Then saith He to Thomas, Reach hither thy finger, and behold My hands; and reach hither thy hand, and thrust it into My side: and be not faithless but believing. And Thomas answered and said unto Him, *My Lord and my God.*"

17

Orchids

1

WE were when he rose from his knees that first Sunday morning after the first Easter Day. A mind like his, so sensitive, so sincere, and so loving, must have been unsparing in self-judgment; the faltering of his faith would not seem a little thing to him. "Let us also go, that we may die with Him," had been his word before. The coldly cautious never speak so. To one who loved his Lord so dearly there must have been grief as well as joy as he heard his Master say, "Because thou hast seen Me thou hast believed: blessed are they that have not seen, and yet have believed." But he had certainty now. Had any questioned him about his faith he would have answered with the assurance of him who wrote,

> Upon a life I did not live,
>   Upon a death I did not die,
> Another's life, Another's death,
>   I stake my whole eternity.

Any faith but one which is fixed in divine revelation seems to me to be like the Indian juggler's rope thrown up in the air. The credulous may believe it can be climbed, they may even "see the juggler do it," or more usually know someone who saw him do it. But he knows that he has never done it and never will. He throws up a rope indeed, but it falls down again. His nearest approach to the impossible is the bamboo trick. He poises a long, slender bamboo pole on hand, or hip, and another man climbs it. A photograph may show the man apparently sitting in air, for the pole is slender, it hardly shows in the sunlight. But a single slip, and the pole falls as certainly as the rope fell.

The thoughts and imagination of our hearts will not carry us far. They are as ropes thrown up into the air. They fall down again. At best they are like the bamboo pole, depending on a fellow man. At any moment they may slip. But there is a ladder set on the earth, and the top of it reaches to heaven. I am the Way, said the Lord Christ.

2

"What new, wonderful thing did you find?" we asked one of our younger boys after his first day in the wooded hills that are our western boundary.

He was silent for a moment, evidently pondering the new, wonderful things of the day; then he said, "Orchids." Orchids crammed in a hothouse (poor things) may appear fantastic rather than beautiful, but at home in their own world they are always the flowers of surprise and of wonder; and the child's heart that lives on in most of us loves a surprise and never loses the sense of wonder. So this rare lady's slipper which grows in shady woods, like the one seen through the window in the wall, shall gather to herself all that a flower may of the lovely element of surprise that waits on wonder and doubles joy.

The spiritual woods where the lover walks are full of the unexpected. The flower of forgetfulness grows there—forgetting the things that are behind "as one experience after another falls behind me into the past." This flower is not blue like the forget-me-not. I see it with a purple bloom upon it, the color of ripe grapes, or yellow, like corn. Joseph found that flower and called his first child after it, Forgetting, "For God, said he, hath made me forget," and his second he called Fruitful, "For God hath caused me to be fruitful." "God's *lethe* is fruitfulness," said Dr. Andrew Bonar.

It is true. Try to recall what caused you to write a date in the margin of your Bible near to some word of strong consolation, and you will find that you remember the consolation but forget the detailed pangs of pain, or, if remembered, they have ceased to be pain: "For God hath made me forget all my toil." It is not just a natural forgetting: "God hath made me forget," and He does most tenderly go on to add to this forgetting, fruit. "Today, when I was having my quiet time," writes a child of this family who is away from home just now, "I came across what I wrote in my private notebook a year ago, and it helped me then, so I shared it with my mother: *For what is it that your Father's tender heart and loving eye looks for first, but the wounded place on which to spend His chiefest care?*"

"The bee is little among such as fly; but her fruit is the chief of sweet things." May this honeybee fly far. But if our little Tara were asked why that drop of honey tasted so sweet to her a year

I think she would find it easier to recall the sweetness of the comfort than the hurt that it healed. There are hurts that ache for years; yet even so it is as though a hand plucked forth the painful sting and restored comforts unto us. And the honey of our comforting is turned into comfort for others. Like the honey in the wood that enlightened the eyes of the weary Jonathan— "Mine eyes have been enlightened because I tasted a little of this honey"—it is used to help God's fighting men.

3

All the great procession of prophets, saints and martyrs, all true warriors of all ages, have found flowers in the wood. St. Paul found them. Perhaps he felt spiritually walled that night in the castle, after the racket and crush of the day, and above all because of the quick word he had flung at his furious enemies like a bone to a pack of dogs, a word which had set them snarling at one another.[13] For the "clever" and the spiritual are poles apart, and the man who is used to breathing the pure air of the heights cannot endure, even for a moment, another, lower air. So St. Paul must have been sad; tired out and very sad. And then, just then, the dearest consolation that could be his was given to him: The Lord stood by him, and said, *Be of good cheer, Paul: for as thou hast testified of Me in Jerusalem so must thou bear witness also at Rome.* He that openeth and no man shutteth had opened a window.

How like our blessed Master this story is. No one who did not know Him could have invented it. Not even in the Land of Flowers shall we find a dearer flower than this which we find when we are tired and sorry, and Love meets us with generous words of cheer, and more—with the last proof of love, the assurance that we are trusted to serve again.

Sometimes we fear lest the voice of a stranger deceive us. "They know not the voice of strangers"—but may not the heart be deceived? Following the manner of Ramon Lull I would quench that fear with very simple words: The Lover asked his Beloved, "How may I know that Thou and not another art speaking with me?" The Beloved answered the Lover, "Would any other bring to thee the comfort that I have brought?"

The Lord make us more like Him in our dealings with souls. The servants are often hard on one another, but never, never is the Master hard. (His words are flames that shrivel insincerity, but that is different.) "Thou hast wrought kindly with Thy servant, O Lord; teach me kindness."[14] Let the prayer of Thy loving Francis of Assisi be my prayer too: "Make me an instrument of Thy peace. Where there is hatred let me sow love, where there is sadness let me sow joy. O Divine Master, grant that I may not so much seek to be consoled, as to console; to be understood, as to understand; to be loved, as to love."

One unkind thought of another, one belittling thought even, unless instantly rejected and forbidden, is enough to bring us crashing down. The outward life of victory is very closely related to the inward life of love.

4

Sometimes the flower of surprise astonishes us by the unexpected way it grows. Orchids do. You look up and see a flash of fire on a brown tree trunk, or a handful of snow where no snow ever fell. On a night of some weariness I came upon an "orchid" called Chimham. "Chimham shall go over"; this unusual title of some verses in an old book caught the eye, and then this note: "Chimham—i.e. , longing, from *kamah*), he longed—a word found only in Psalm 63:1, My flesh longeth for Thee." Barzillai the Gileadite could not go over the river with David. "But behold my son Chimham, let him go over with my lord the king." So it does not matter that we must wait for a while in Gilead. "Our 'Longing' shall go over, and dwell, O Lord, with Thee."

Many of our South Indian orchids are very small, smaller than violets and even more inconspicuous, and yet one treasures them. That kind of little joy, treasured ever since, was found (or given, rather) the first time I was "doolied" up the Ghats. It was before the days of hill railway and motor; four coolies swung the traveler up the lovely mountain road, crooning as they ran at a steady jog-trot one of their ancient chanties called a *yélum*, because of its refrain, *Yé, lé, lum, yé, lé, lé, lum.*

It was an inspiring prospect that opened with every bend of the road, for though the mountains were steep they rose from a sunlit valley, and the air was full of the sweet noise of birds' songs and whistles and calls, and the flowing of waters murmuring somewhere under the green. But I was not inspired. My breakdown in Japan had not encouraged the doctors to pass me for India. And now in this my first hot weather, "I give her six months," said a hopeful medical worker. But I had thought my call was for life. To add to the depression of the hour there was the flatness that comes after fever; and the doubtless true but rather melancholy lines slipped into the *yélum* tune and sighed themselves over monotonously.

> Thou shalt need all the strength that God can give,
> Simply to live, my friend, simply to live.

Then suddenly like the blue flash of a kingfisher's wing, like the quick flight of a flock of little birds, these words came flying through the wood: *"I have as much grace for you as I have green for My trees."* And I knew that our Father had spoken to me as one might speak to a child.

The green of millions of trees, green as South Indian forests can be—fold upon fold of green velvet spread upon the mountains, vast and limitless like the sea—this was the setting of the new *yélum*. It was an inexhaustible word. I have often thanked our Lord of Love for that word. O Jesus, Lover of Thy least lovable, most foolish, least useful little child, we Thy little children thank Thee. Thou hast as much grace for us as Thou hast green for Thy trees, grace to help in time of need. Thou canst make something of the least of us. Thou canst make us to be "life, fire, wing, force."

5

There is no end to the variety of these orchids of God. A missionary wife and mother who was preparing to sail for Africa found something she will never forget in an unusual text. She and her family are not very good sailors, and she was "a little bit anxious about having to travel third class this time. It was one morning, one of our last mornings at home. While I was praying there came the words, *And He was in the hinder part of the ship,* and I knew they were from Him to me; and after that the hinder part was the only place in the whole boat for me, and the inward comfort was complete."

"*Pure olive oil beaten for the light, to cause the lamp to burn always*" (that the lamp may lift up its flame continually, as Rotherham has it) came to me once on a dark evening. Olive berries, bruised, crushed out of semblance of berries; oil beaten out, pure oil; their flame lifted up continually, living flame. It is clear picture-language, a figure of the true.

And with those words came this, *Ye are they which have continued with Me in My temptations.* It is the word above all others, I think, that we should most dearly love our Lord to say to us. And He answers the thought of the heart before it forms in words: "Everyone when he is perfected shall be as his Master." "I am that maketh thee to long: I it am, the endless fulfilling of all true desires."

6

All true desires? Perhaps the word will take you, if you are ill or disabled, to a deep dell in the orchid wood, where for a while the air is quiet, and then, it may be, a clamor of voices will break upon you, and you will be rent with longings to *do* again. To serve the children of your love has been the joy of your life, and you cannot serve them now. They are upon your heart when you go in before the Lord, but, oh, to be able to *do* with hands and feet and all that there is of you, once more! O Lord, how long? And you lie down tired out with desire. But this is not the end of that hour in the dell.

The hush of a Presence, a sound of gentle stillness, a Voice you recognize: *"My child, what was I doing when I was nailed upon the cross?"*

Then you see as we see a landscape in a dream, all Palestine spread at His feet. Cities, villages, crowded with sick folk whom

He could have healed, sad folk whom He could have comforted; and He could not heal them, could not comfort them, could not move one little inch towards them; and He loved them, had lived to serve them, and the whole multitude had sought to touch Him, for there went virtue out of Him and healed them all—and now?

"Then said I, Lo, I come, in the volume of the book it is written of Me, *I delight to do Thy will, O my God: yea, Thy law is within my heart.*" The mysterious words rise slowly, one by one; His own words are the answer to His question. And the words are alight, like the lamp in the sanctuary that lifted up its flame continually. In that light you see your calling, and you hear the voice you love best in all the world: "*What then, My child, of thee?*"

But He was pouring out His soul unto death, and bearing the sin of many, and making intercession for the transgressors—there is not any comparison between what He was doing then and what you are doing now. No, there is not any comparison. And yet He calls you into the fellowship of a new way of obedience. Lo, I come—to do Thy *will*, O my God. And the lovely old words of the Great Bible of our forefathers fall softly on the ear, "I am content to do it."

Always bearing about in the body the dying of the Lord Jesus that the life also of Jesus might be made manifest in our body— that is the call now: "Far was the call and farther as I followed . . . grew there a silence around my Lord and me."

7

Often this orchid of the deep wood is private between the Beloved and His lover. It is some secret of the Lord, some "secret converse," like the "secret ministries which ripen the corn and make the wild flowers perfect in form and hue, where no eye of man shall ever see them."

Such ministries must be folded up in quietness; we must "learn to love softly." The friend who knows nothing of reticence finds himself in the outer courts of his friend's house; he becomes a stranger to him, and in his house also his friend is a stranger. There is not between them now the *colloquium familiare*, as Gesenius translates "secret" in Psalm 25:14. The courtesies of life may continue, but that is all. They drift apart. They are never at home any more with one another.

It is a sadness that cannot be told when this happens between friends. It is as the shadow of death to the lover of the Lord when, by some careless holding of a treasure given in trust, he loses that which he had before, that intimate "sweet talking, much wonderful familiarity," which was common and oft with the inward man, and sees his Beloved pass his house, as though He were only a stranger. But let the heart hasten after Him, let it care for nothing but to recall its Lord, its Love, its alone Master, and He will allow Himself to be recalled. For it grieves Him to be as a stranger and as a wayfaring man who turneth aside to tarry for a night. He desires to be constrained. O divine humility of love—He waits to be constrained by our desire.

Dear Lord, we constrain Thee now. Abide with us: for it is toward evening and the day is far spent. Come in and tarry with us. Do not vanish out of our sight. "Come not to sojourn, but abide with me." Let there be even for me once more the *colloquium familiare* of love.

18

Veils

1

THERE is peace in the picture. "Those words, peace, silence, rest, and the others, take on a vividness in the midst of noise and worry and weariness, like lighted windows in the dark":

> Sleepe after toyle, port after stormie seas,
> Ease after warre, death after life, doth greatly please.

The picture has the look of evening, but it belongs to any hour of the day's life. There is no need to wait till sunset to behold with open face as in a glass the glory of the Lord. The vexations which may harass even morning hours need not make a veil between the soul and its sun.

There is nothing of light in the rock; it is as other rocks. But it is bathed in light. As so often in a picture, it is the light that makes the difference. ("And because my thought so shone, I knew she had been shone upon.") Even on a dark and cloudy day, if our inward beholding be not hindered we shall be surprised by sudden lightenings,

> Radiance that comes we know not how nor whence;
> Rainbows without rain, past duller sense.

It is of no account that we are naught. He shines upon His dust and His dust shines.

But if there be a dimness, not a shining, is it because we see too much of man and too little of our Master? We cannot make His way known to others unless we abide in the light of His countenance. To be with our fellow servants is not enough. "Tell me, O Thou whom my soul loveth, where Thou feedest, where Thou makest Thy flock to rest at noon: for why should I he as one that turneth aside by the flocks of Thy companions?"

2

Many things can weave veils between us and our dear Lord. "I feared a fear and it came upon me," came upon me like a mist, came between me and my light. The way to tear that veil to shreds is to do what Gideon did when he took the word of his God quite simply, and gave a peaceful name to the place of his fear: Gideon said, "Alas, O Lord God!" And the Lord said unto him, "Peace be unto thee; fear not, thou shalt not die." Then Gideon built an altar there unto the Lord, and called it Jehovah-Shalom, *The Lord is peace*. The place of my fear becomes the place of my peace. I am out of rest when I fear. Return unto thy rest, O my soul; for the Lord hath dealt bountifully with thee.

Theories about disaster or trial, the varying judgments of people and their conclusions—each separate thread of talk can contribute a thread towards the weaving of a veil. Texts used without reference to context can darken the very sun.

To take the words about chastening in Hebrews 12 to ourselves is one thing; to give them as a matter of course to another is, I think, different. For what if that other be an Epaphroditus?[15] He could have avoided this that has come to him by caring a little more for himself, a little less for his Lord; a careful, cool, calculating love never leads to the place where Epaphroditus is so often found.

When we are paralyzed by our soul's surrenderings, and our hands hang down and our knees are feeble, and the paths that we make for our feet are crooked, and the lame are turned out of the way, then the Shining One of the Pilgrim's story comes with a whip of small cord in his hand. "And as he chastised them, he said, As many as I love I rebuke and chasten; be zealous therefore and repent." And this chastening was not meant to be "joyous, but grievous." But the Shining One did not go on scourging the pilgrims indefinitely. "This done, he bids them go on their way, so they thanked him for all his kindness, and went softly along the right way singing." It is a perfect illustration of Hebrews 12.

But there are other pilgrims, the little and the innocent, who for no turning aside of their own have a suffering childhood; there are those too, and they are many, for whom the book of Job and certain psalms and large portions of the New Testament were written.

And there is Epaphroditus—a name dear to God, for the Lord loveth a hilarious giver, and the happy word expresses that happy soul. We have all known Epaphroditus. We have seen him "playing as it were, the gambler with his life." We have seen him pay for that glad hour through long, slow months—perhaps years; for he is a soldier, and his Captain never promised him immunity from the hazards of battle. (Would such a promise have attracted him?) But the fighting man of old days, shot by the archers because he was near to his Captain, at whom those archers perpetually did shoot, was not accustomed to make much of his wound. Right glad was he that he was near enough to his Captain to stop an arrow on its way to him. And Epaphroditus does not think much of the ills that come because, not regarding his life, he was allowed to supply some lack of service to his dear Lord. He sees them rather as gifts: "Unto you it is given in the behalf of Christ, not only to believe on Him, but also to suffer for His sake."

A word like this, *to you it is given*, takes the ache from battle wounds. It leaves Epaphroditus humbly happy instead of half bewildered, half brokenhearted by the thought that somehow, somewhere he must be grieving his Lord and so compelling Him to continue to "scourge" him. It quiets his heart, it opens his ear to other words: "Count it all joy, beloved, think it not strange. To him that overcometh will I give to eat of the hidden manna, and will give him a white stone, and in the stone a new name written, which no man knoweth, saving he that receiveth it." But what these words mean it has not entered into the heart of Epaphroditus to imagine, even in a dream.

3

Veils are thin things, and can be woven from very fine threads; such a trifle as the kind of night that makes a golden text of the words "There shall be no night there" can be a busy weaver. "Oh, how different is battle from the speculations of those who meditate amid the columns of the cloister!" Many have echoed that Crusader. Nothing could have allured us from our field. Had anyone tried to persuade us to consider some cleaner, nicer, brighter sphere, we would have turned on him:

Yours are only the drum and the fife,
The golden braid and the surface of life;
Ours is the red-hot war.

But now that the wave of war has swept us up on some deserted shore where there is nothing to do (as it seems) but suffer a while, it is different. We can pray? When we can, we are more than content. But there are times when we cannot; at least, we cannot attempt sustained prayer. We are often unhappily conscious that we are believed to be praying more than we truly are. For we cannot gather our thoughts to pray; they scatter like a flock of goats on an Indian road which has neither hedge nor ditch, and we cannot run after them. Discouragement will try to turn weaver then.

It is good to remember that we are not alone on this barren coast; like every other form of temptation, this that afflicts us is common to man. If others have found a way of peace here, we may. Jesus called a little child unto Him and set him in the midst of them. Set a little child in the midst of your thoughts. See it when it is ill. It cannot say much to its mother, but it can "look" its love, and the mother understands. The frequent little looks of love passing between mother and child, the frequent little touches of love, these are the signs of love. The Maker of mothers is not less understanding than the mothers He has made. "O more than mother's heart, I come, a weary child, to Thee."

And as we come a score of times a day, and as often by night, perhaps not so much praying as just looking, remembering ("I will remember Thee upon my bed"), now and then will rise unbidden "sweet words according to the feeling, either loving or worshiping or wondering, or otherwise sounding as the heart liketh." And He whom our soul loveth "showeth His privy jewels, much thing He giveth and more He promiseth, and courteous dalliance He showeth."

4

In that courteous dalliance the inmost thoughts of the heart are understood and answered. You had hoped to burn out, not rust out. You had expected (if the Lord tarried) the natural end of the fighting man. And now you are lapped in softness. You look back at a certain moment which changed everything. But "moment" is too long a word; was it a period of time at all? There came a thunderclap. But no, thunder may rumble for two or three seconds. This was a lightning-flash cleaving straight across the road on which you walked. You shut your eyes instinctively; when you opened them the road looked different. And it was different. Nothing will ever be again as it was before that lightning-flash. This, and this, and this you will never do again. And the road will grow duller and darker with every mile you go—is that your thought?

A Voice speaks within you:

"Things will never be as they were before? That is true; for they will be better.

"You will never do this and this again? That also is true; for I have other things for you to do.

"They are not what you would choose? But they are indeed the best that Love can choose for you.

"The road will grow duller and darker with every mile you go? The path is like a shining light; like the sun that you have watched on many a lovely morning coming out of his chambers and rejoicing as a strong man to run a race. Does the light on that shining racecourse of the sky grow less and less? No, it shineth more and more. So shall the path of My beloved be, not darker, but brighter as it nears the perfect day. This is the heritage of the servants of the Lord. *This*, not that."

And yet—O Lord, forgive; the things I cannot do are looking in through my window now, and beckoning me, and calling me.

"But I am here in the room with you: I am nearer than those beckoning, calling things. I come between them and you. You have nothing to do, now, but to please Me." Then, though you may have been trained in the noblest liturgy on earth, you echo the simple words as a young child might, *"I have nothing to do now, but to please Thee."* And Thou art not hard to please, O blessed Lover of us all.

There are days when the Lord whom we adore comes marching upon the great highways of life; as a Leader and Commander of His people He comes, as a refuge from the storm, a shadow from the heat when the blast of the terrible ones is as a storm against the wall. And all the voices of the world sound forth like the notes of a mighty organ, "Trust ye in the Lord for ever: for in the Lord Jehovah is everlasting strength." And there are other days when He comes walking without sound or footfall in our gardens. We hear Him then in whispers, softer than the whisper of a light wind on the grass; we know Him present as we know the presence of a fragrant flower in the room—a flower that we cannot see.

> Lord God of gardens, who in love disposes
>   Sun, rain, wind violent,
> So that our bushes flower to Thee in roses,
>   We are content.
>
> We do not ask to choose our garden's weather,
>   Too ignorant are we—
> Only that we, Thy gardeners, together
>   May pleasure Thee.

5

But is this a shining path? The question is sure to come even if we are only going through the lesser ills of life, and if it be the greater, the kind that wrings soul or body with giant hands, that question will come with tremendous force. Is this a path that shineth more and more unto the perfect day? Is to live like this to bring our Lord anything worth offering? Or is such writing a mere jumble of words—a religious lie, most despicable of lies?

It is not a lie; it is true. We do not build our faith on the baseless fabric of a dream. Pretty fictions are brittle toys. And yet the seen and the felt crowd upon us so mercilessly, and crush us so, that it can be very difficult honestly to believe that things are different in reality from what they appear to be. We cannot see a path that shines. We cannot see anything in our life, lived as it must be now, that can possibly give pleasure to our Lord.

But continually we look at things about. us without seeing more than a very little of what is there. We look up into the sky at noon and know that familiar constellations are passing over us, but we do not see them. Empty blue, or grey, or masses of cloud—that is all we see. We look at a pool or any little runlet of softly flowing water; we are looking into fairyland; but we do not catch even a flutter of a fairy scarf. Water and the reflections and colors on its surface—that is all we see. We know that we see in part where the material world is concerned. Why should we not be comforted where the spiritual is in question by remembering that there also we see only in part? We dwell perpetually in the presence of far more than we can see. Our feelings say, "How can this thing be good?" But if God declares it is, that is enough. And as we follow on to know the Lord we learn that our puny circumstances shall never defy the powers of quickening Love. And Love kindles faith. And Love strengthens faith. And Love nourishes the full assurance of hope. And then Love leads us into prayer.

For Love is always saying, "Seek ye My face"; and our hearts are always answering, "Thy face, Lord, will I seek." But even as we seek, pressing through the outer courts of the House to behold the beauty of the Lord and to enquire in His temple, we are beset by a question, perhaps by a doubt that waits on the very threshold of the House, seeking to confound us as we would enter in: How can our prayer, so fitful, so interrupted, so weighted, so far from what we want it to be, rise to that pure place where His honor dwelleth? "Hear Thou in heaven Thy dwelling-place: and when Thou hearest, forgive"—gratefully we use the words. "Thou art the same Lord whose property is always to have mercy. . . . Not weighing our merits but pardoning our offences." But He has so much to pardon; only our hearts know how much. And there are no merits to weigh, nor ever can be.

Our heavenly Father often answers our questions as we answer our children's, in plain words; but sometimes He takes us into "that higher world where metaphor, as we know it, is the very stuff of life." His plain words about prayer are our familiar friends, but we may have missed the comfort that is in St. John's vision of the angel who came and stood at the altar, having a golden censer. And there was given unto him much incense that he should offer it with the prayers of all saints upon the golden altar which was before the throne. And the smoke of the incense, which came with the prayers of the saints (forgiven sinners, whom Love names so) ascended up before God out of the angel's hand. Those prayers that we know were so poor are cared for as something of value. They are put in golden bowls, and with them is mixed the Much Incense of the merits of our Lord.

I did not fully understand the divine simplicity of the words "And the smoke of the incense, which came with the prayers of the saints, ascended up before God out of the angel's hand," till I saw incense used, as it has been from time immemorial in India, in simple household ways. You throw a few grains on burning charcoal and a column of smoke rises straight up. Anyone coming into the room notices the fragrance long after the smoke has disappeared. It fills the room, floats out through the open doors and windows, and for an hour or so, if the air be still, you are aware of it about the house. I never watch that white column of smoke, laden with its own peculiar fragrance, without a grateful thought about that of which it is the figure. There is nothing in our prayers that would cause them to rise. But they are cleansed and perfumed and lifted. It is all of Him who ever liveth to make intercession for us. It is all of Him who is our one eternal radiance:

O Love of loves, we have no good to bring Thee,
    No single good of all our hands have wrought.
No worthy music have we found to sing Thee,
    No jeweled word, no quick up-soaring thought.

And yet we come; and when our faith would falter
    Show us, O Lord, the quiet place of prayer,
The golden censer and the golden altar,
    And the great angel waiting for us there.

And now for today, in this room, ward, workshop, house; in city or in village, or in ship upon the sea; in our going forth with others or endurance out of sight, in the "now" and "here" of common life, may we not make a pause for adoration? Our Lord is too little adored: To Him who is "above all the knighthood of heaven" be glory. Blessing, and glory, and wisdom, and thanksgiving, and honor, and power, and might, be unto our God forever and ever. Therefore with angels and archangels, and with all the company of heaven, we laud and magnify Thy glorious Name; evermore praising Thee, and saying, Holy, holy, holy, Lord God of hosts, heaven and earth are full of Thy glory: Glory be to Thee, O Lord most high.

19

Must

1

HERE is an under-passion in life—in a life, at least, that confronts leagued fiends.

God, fight we not within a cursed world,
Whose very air teems thick with leagued fiends—
Be earnest, earnest, earnest,

but to the outward eye our days are made of a stream of minutes spent in doing common duties, spent in suffering too with those who suffer.

"I have a baptism to be baptized with; and how am I straitened till it be accomplished! . . . Are ye able to drink of the cup that I shall drink of, and to be baptized with the baptism that I am baptized with? They said unto Him, We are able. And He saith unto them, Ye shall drink indeed of My cup and be baptized with the baptism that I am baptized with. . . . The Son of Man came not to be ministered unto, but to minister, and to give His life a ransom for many." It is in the fellowship of this ministry that the cup must be drunk and the baptism accepted. A great Must dominated the life of the Son of Man. That Must will dominate ours if we follow in His footsteps. "No one of you who does not detach himself from all that belongs to him can be a disciple of Mine," said the Master.[16]

We shall feel sometimes like this battered pine, thrashed by the wind. "Each snarling blast shot through me." That tree is like a soul hard beset and alone so far as human companionship is concerned. *"Every strong conviction ends by taking possession of us; it overcomes and absorbs us, and tears us ruthlessly from everything else; it becomes our sole object, and outside it nothing seems to touch us; those who do not understand it are strangers to us; those who attack it are our enemies; those who love and serve it with us are our true, our only family."*

That true, that only family is the dear possession of those who count all well lost for the sake of the one supreme purpose which dominates life. To be one of such a family means not living upon the joy of fellowship: there must always be inward detachment, for companionship in the flesh is not promised. Many a thought of God has been hindered (to use the speech of earth) because two friends refused to separate. But even though it may not be a question of vocation, a loyal allegiance holds the heart of the Lord's lover. If his nearest are not one in that allegiance, there will be times when he is very lonely, for there is no loneliness so acute as loneliness in a crowd.

Sometimes the weaning of the child (the training that teaches it to do without) is like a cold sharp wind. We needed a prop at first, and we were given one. We leaned; we loved to lean. And then it was taken away:

> Gently loosens He thy hold
>   Of the treasured former things,
> Loves and joys that were of old,
>   Shapes to which the spirit clings.

The words were written in days when a man who loved his Lord enough to obey Him was persecuted as a fanatic. It may be those days are coming again. Perhaps they have come. Certain it is that the reason there is so much shallow living—much talk, but little obedience—is that so few are prepared to be, like the pine on the hilltop, alone in the wind for God.

For life is not a gay affair like the skimming of a yacht on summer seas. If we are in earnest to set our hearts on the greatest things—likeness to our Lord, abandonment to His service with no ends of our own—we shall not find it so. "Beware what you set your heart upon, for it surely shall be yours"; beware of the insincere in prayer. "The Lord remember all thy offerings and turn to ashes thy burnt sacrifice" (Psalm 20:3. See the Geneva Bible.). A sacrifice accepted is a sacrifice consumed.

•   •   •

There was a pause in the temple worship after that prayer was offered. We often hasten on to the next petition, "Grant thee according to thine own heart, and fulfill all thy counsel" (vs. 4). But the soul cannot be hurried. There must be a *Selah*. In that pause we see the divine "must" of suffering. "I will show him what great things he must suffer for My sake"—not what great things he must do, achieve, enjoy.

There may be a long interval between the two clauses, "Ask and ye shall receive . . . that your joy may be full." But the end of true prayer is always joy. The sorrow is turned into joy. This is more than to have a cup emptied of sorrow and filled with joy. The sorrow itself is transformed even as the earthly garments that our Saviour wore became shining and white as the light when He was transfigured on the mountain.

Our joy shall be full when we see what Eternal Wisdom wrought for us through the difficult days of time. And throughout those days the soul that refuses to be offended is marvelously comforted. The Father draws His shattered child very close to His heart. The secret of the Lord is with them that fear Him and He will show them His covenant, that covenant of peace that shall never be removed.

For the turning to ashes is only one side of the truth. The other is shown in that beautiful figure of the true—Aaron's rod, that budded, and brought forth buds, and bloomed blossoms, and yielded almonds. Perhaps the reason that we know so little of the deeper things of prayer is that we know so little of the Selah between those two verses of the twentieth psalm.

This book may fall into the hands of one to whom the "must" of a divine constraint is no dream of imagination but a tremendous fact. To his "Friends will miss me, they say," his Lord has answered, "Choose ye tonight if I am to miss you or they." He cannot argue with those who do not understand, he cannot explain, only he knows that he must obey. "How am I straitened till it be accomplished"—it is like that. No other way is possible for him. He has passed the place where the road forks. He cannot go back on his call. He cannot resist the constraint.

Then in God's name, I say, *Let him yield to it: let him go on.* The storm will beat upon him. He must be prepared for that. "Woe unto you when all men speak well of you"—he may have to learn the meaning of that uncoveted word. "Blessed are *ye poor*"—he may have to taste of that blessedness; not many desire it. He may have to stand alone on his hilltop like that stone pine. "The soul would endure splendid martyrdoms, but her Lord lays upon her the ultimate reward of failure and of death"—the ultimate reward? Yes and no. Beyond the Seen is the Unseen. *That* is the ultimate reward.

For always that which gives imperishable gold to a life (as to a book) is not the trend of the opinions which direct its course, not its success—never its success; it is the steadfastness and the integrity of its spirit, the love which inspires it, the note of the eternal which dominates it.

2

The Son of Man must. And so His followers must. The storm must beat upon them as they seek to serve. "Verily, verily I say unto you, Except a corn of wheat fall into the ground and die, it abideth alone: but if it die, it bringeth forth much fruit"; this is the same truth under another figure. What didst Thou ask of life, Lord Jesus, Lord of Life? "No victor's crown, but only wood enough to make a cross." The Son of Man must suffer many things:

> In patience, as in labor, must thou be
>   A follower of Me,
> Whose hands and feet,
> when most I wrought for thee,
>   Were nailed unto a Tree.

"And so we come to Thee; O Thou that hearest prayer, unto Thee shall all flesh come. From the end of the earth will I cry unto Thee, when my heart is overwhelmed: lead me to the rock that is higher than I."

Looking up from the shelter of that rock, we hear words that fall quietly one by one, even as the stars drop through the dim blue, till almost before we know it, the sky is full of stars: "Peace I leave with you, My peace I give unto you: not as the world giveth, give I unto you. Let not your heart be troubled, neither let it be afraid." Our hearts are quiet then: "I trust to rest in Thy great hallowing."

By such gentle ways we are led till we come to the place where we understand that it is not enough to accept the will of our God in the sense of ceasing to wish it were different, and taking it peacefully. We must go further than that. We are not wholly loyal till we learn to welcome it. Stormy wind fulfilling His word—by the time the wind blows upon us it is His wind for us. We have nothing to do with what first of all stirred up that wind. It could not ruffle a leaf on the smallest tree in the forest had He not opened the way for it to blow through the fields of air. He commandeth even the winds, and they obey Him. To His winds as to His servants He saith to one "Go," and it goeth; and to another "Come," and it cometh; and to another

"Do this," and it doeth it. So whatever wind blows on us it is His wind for us, His wind fulfilling His word. Therefore not to welcome it is a kind of treachery.

God's winds do an effectual work. They utterly blow away from us what *The Spirit of Discipline* calls the meanness and vulgarity of self-satisfaction; the absurdity of self-centeredness and self-advertisement; the ludicrous littleness of unreality, and all acquiescence in poor and stunted thoughts of life. They shake loose from us the things that can be shaken, that those things which cannot be shaken may remain, those eternal things that belong to the Kingdom which cannot be moved. They have their part to play in stripping us and strengthening us so that we may be the more ready for the uses of Eternal Love. Then can we refuse to welcome them?

"The lover asked his Beloved if there remained in him anything still to be loved. And the Beloved replied *that he had still to love that by which his own love could be increased.*" O my Redeemer and my Lord, Thou dost often increase love by that which is very lovable, but sometimes Thou comest otherwise. I cannot by nature love that which is unlovable to me. Do Thou for me, O God the Lord, do Thou for me. "Give me what Thou commandest and command what Thou wilt." Cause me to know the way wherein I should walk; cause me to love that way, so that in me love may be perfected, and I be made more serviceable to my Beloved.

•　　•　　•

"Art thou indeed willing, O child of My desire? Art thou willing for any wind at any time? Art thou willing to lose thy life that thou mayest find it? Then hush thy heart to listen as I make intercession for thee.

"Father, I will that they also, whom Thou hast given Me, be with Me where I am: that they may behold My glory, which Thou hast given Me; for Thou lovedst Me before the foundation of the world. And I have declared unto them Thy name, and will declare it: that the love wherewith Thou hast loved Me may be in them, and I in them."

The love wherewith the Father loved the Son was a love which gave His Son to Calvary.

3

Calvary, the word pierces even to the dividing asunder of soul and spirit. It is a discerner of the thoughts and intents of the heart. It searches our love for our beloved. It discovers the quality of that love. An Indian refiner puts his glistening gold into a small earthen crucible. As he blows up the fire, grey scum floats to the surface of the gold. The grey scum of selfishness in our human love will float to the surface of our soul and be discovered by us, if we are willing to allow the Refiner to blow up His fire. There is a rooted possessiveness about much of human affection. "My loved one for myself"—that is the underlying thought of much that looks so beautiful.

God's thought was different. The love that our Lord asks for us is different. His Father's love was a giving love.

Often the children in a Christian family are ready and eager to follow their Lord all the way, but the parents pull them back. A few rise to the heights of not refusing them. Their high-water mark is expressed is such words as these:

> O Father, help, lest our poor love refuse
> For our beloved the life that they would choose,
> And in our fear of loss for them, or pain,
>   Forget eternal gain.

For some even that has seemed high. But the love of God infinitely passes that. With Him it was never that He did not refuse; it was that He gave the Son of His love unto death, "even the death of the cross." What do we know of sacrificial love?

Ignatius Loyola knew it, and his earlier followers knew it: "Set the Indies on fire, Francisco," he said as he sent his young disciple to a service that was to see nothing of ease, and never a furlough, till on the edge of China his warfare was accomplished.

Count Zinzendorf knew it, and his Moravians knew it: "I have one passion; it is Christ and Him only." Because that passion consumed him he could lead the parents of his community into the joy of the giver who holds nothing back. *Have we as a Church lost the power to lead others into sacrificial giving? Have I lost the power to lead those committed to me? Was it ever mine at all?* We cannot lead the climber further than we have gone ourselves. We cannot inspire the soldier to storm the fort from which we have fallen back. We cannot even point to a heavenly vision which, having seen ourselves, we have disregarded. "Whereupon, O king Agrippa, I was not disobedient unto the heavenly vision"— and the loyal and obedient spirit of his leader set Timothy on fire.

Where have we failed?

When our Lord spoke of His Father's love He knew His Father's heart. He knew as no created being can know, the utmost reaches of the love wherewith His Father loved Him, the utmost reaches of that bleak land of pain to which that love had given Him.

And yet on the evening of His betrayal He did not desire for us the less costly love, the natural love which shrinks from a hard way for a beloved one and never contemplates anything approaching shame. Human love with its loopholes of escape from the supreme demand was not in His mind. It was divine love that He desired should be in us, the love wherewith He Himself was loved, divine love with all its agonizing possibilities—but with great certainty of eternal joy. We have lowered the standard. That which should be usual has become so unusual that we are surprised and stirred, and write books about these bright particular stars in our firmament who have shone mightily in loving. Such lives should be the rule, the others the exception. Have we in our refusal of the crucifix refused also the cross? We do refuse the crucifix. The sign of our faith, as Westcott said long ago, is an empty cross, an empty tomb: He is not here, He is risen. But it is strangely possible to decorate that empty cross, to smother it in flowers, even (but surely this borders on blasphemy) to use the symbol as an ornament. And yet the great law stands: "Whosoever doth not bear his cross, and come after Me, cannot be My disciple."

We who follow the Crucified are not here to make a pleasant thing of life; we are called to suffer for the sake of a suffering, sinful world. The Lord forgive us our shameful evasions and hesitations. His brow was crowned with thorns; do we seek rosebuds for our crowning? His hands were pierced with nails; are our hands ringed with jewels? His feet were bare and bound; do our feet walk delicately? What do we know of travail? of tears that scald before they fall? of heartbreak? of being scorned? God forgive us our love of ease. God forgive us that so often we turn our faces from a life that is even remotely like His. Forgive us that we all but worship comfort, the delight of the presence of loved ones, possessions, treasure on earth. Far, far from our prayers too often is any thought of prayer for a love which will lead us to give one whom we love to follow our Lord to Gethsemane, to Calvary—perhaps because we have never been there ourselves.

Lord, we kneel beside Thee now, with hands folded between Thy hands as a child's are folded in its mother's. We would follow the words of Thy prayer, dimly understanding their meaning, but wanting to understand. . . . *"That the love wherewith Thou hast loved Me may be in them, and I in them."*

20

Fortitude

1

THIS photograph of mountain stone pines, so fretted with the gusts of heaven and yet so resolutely rooted, is not here for its beauty, for a broken tree is not beautiful, but because it shows God's "children of tempest" who shall be found unshaken in the Morning. Spare me the stub of a sword; let me fight on to the end—that is its word.

"Die hard, my men, die hard!" shouted Colonel Inglis of the 57th to his men on the heights behind the river Albuhera. The regiment was nicknamed the Die-hards after that. The tale may have been forgotten but the name lives on, and in spite of foolish uses it is a great name. It challenges us. We are called to be the Lord's Die-hards to whom can be committed any kind of trial of endurance, and who can be counted upon to stand firm whatever happens. It is written of Cromwell: "He strove to give his command so strict a unity that in no crisis should it crack." With this aim in view he made his Ironsides. The result of that discipline was seen not only in victory but in defeat; for his troops, "though they were beaten and routed, presently rallied again and stood in good order till they received new orders."[17]

This is the spirit that animates all valiant life: to be strong in will—to strive, to seek, to find, and not to yield—is all that ever matters. Failure or success, as the world understands these words, is of no eternal account. To be able to stand steady in defeat is in itself a victory. There is no tinsel about that kind of triumph.

Wind means stress and strain. "The elastic limit" of each kind of tree is known to the engineer, and he deals accordingly with his timber. So does the Creator of the trees, the Commander of the winds, know "the elastic limit" of His several trees. And He knows the weight of the winds. "He looketh to the ends of the earth, to make the weight for the winds."

> When He appointed to the wind its weight,
> And weighed the water according to a measure,
> When He appointed to the rain its law,
> And the course to the lightning of the thunder;
> Then He saw it and declared it,
> Took it as a pattern and tested it also.[18]

The weight of the winds can be tremendous. Here is one who has great gifts of mind but who, because of some structural trouble in the head, cannot read or listen to reading. To be free from severe and persistent pain only when utterly quiescent, and yet to be kept in peace, is surely something very greatly to the glory of His grace. Here is another, shattered, paralyzed and blinded. That wind can tear the branches from the pine. "Nothing but the Infinite Pity is sufficient for the infinite pathos of human life," but that is only half a truth. *Nothing but the courageous Love of God is brave enough to trust the soul of man to endure as seeing Him who is invisible; and nothing but the grace of God can carry that soul through in triumph.*

There is no promise that all shall be made easy. There will be days when the smallest fret, a jarring noise, the chatter of voices in visiting hours in a hospital ward, bustling people, people who drum on the rail of the bed, or knock it, or drop things, a crooked picture, wrong colors put together, a book upside down, something perversely lost among the bedclothes, will be absurdly but intensely irritating. Even common good temper will need to be prayed for then; it will not come of itself.

"For ye have need of patience: let patience have her perfect work." On such a day, as many could tell, these twin words have a gentle habit of walking hand in hand into the room, rather like shy children, not quite sure of their welcome but hoping you will be kind to them. You remember another word then (though it seems too much to believe it will ever be spoken to you), *"I know thy patience and how thou hast borne and hast not fainted."* And so you are reminded of your high calling. There is a curious comfort in remembering that the Father depends upon His child not to give way. It is inspiring to be trusted with a hard thing. You never asked for summer breezes to blow upon your tree. It is enough that you are not alone upon the hill.

2

There is a page in the story *Mr. Standfast* which makes bracing reading in windy weather. It helps to toughen fiber. Dick Hannay, so the tale runs, has a letter from his friend Peter Pienaar, who was having a stiff fight with himself. He was trying to keep his courage going in face of the bitterest trial he could be called on to face, a crippled old age.

He writes first of ordinary bravery, "I mean by being brave, playing the game by the right rules without letting it worry you that you may very likely get knocked on the head." That kind of courage, he says, is only good nerves and experience. "But the big courage is the cold-blooded kind, the kind that never lets go even when you're feeling empty inside, and your blood's thin, and there's no kind of fun or profit to be had, and the trouble's not over in an hour or two but lasts for months and years. One of the men here was speaking about that kind and he called it 'Fortitude.' I reckon fortitude's the biggest thing a man can have—just to go on enduring when there's no guts or heart left in you." And Peter went on enduring, nourished upon the strong meat he found in his two only books, his Bible and his *Pilgrim's Progress*; and he wins through and makes a gallant end. But his friend does not see that end, "for my eyes were blinded and I was on my knees."

There are certain winds of adversity which can wither every green thing and tear up every rooted thing (unless there be this fortitude), and there is no choice about whether those winds shall blow or not: "For the love of God thou oughtest to suffer all things, labors, and sorrows, temptations, vexations, anxieties, necessities, infirmities, wrongs, obloquies, reprehensions, humiliations, confusions, corrections, and despites. These things helpeth to virtue, these prove the knight of Christ, these make the heavenly crown."

3

Obloquies, most hateful of all wind of words: there is a tradition that Annas and Caiaphas brought a charge against our Lord about His nativity. A coarse word refers to His "holy" birth and a cruel word to the massacre of the Innocents. One who has lived a lifetime in the East sees in such a tradition the hallmark of truth. But He had more to bear. It is impossible that His mother was sheltered from this cutting wind. For her, obloquy was the thrust of the sword. What must it have been to her Son to see that sword pierce through her own soul also?

There is no painful road on which He has not walked; He is always farther on that road than we have gone: "They laid to my charge things that I knew not." Our roughest storm appears a zephyr when we think of the hurricanes that beat upon Him. Even the grief of seeing the staff whereon we leaned snap under sudden strain (and the splinter always pierces our hand), even the shock of finding one whom we had thought flint turn into a man of straw, and the twist of pain which wrings out the cry

"It was not an enemy: then I could have borne it. But it was thou!"—even that poignant grief He knew to the uttermost. "Ah, but the treason of friends, their shiftiness, their suspicion, their doubt, their withdrawal—therein lies real suffering. Those who have never felt that have felt nothing, have never suffered even a scratch," wrote the discredited Didon. The Sinless One walked that road.

Consider Him who endured. The word has a tranquilizing power. The endurance which "remains under," which does not try to slip from under or to float over and so escape from the trial—that is what we see when we consider our Lord, so marred, more than any man, and His form more than the sons of men, and yet eternal Lover of men, eternal Conqueror.

But if we are to "remain under" and triumph in our lesser trials, so that in the end we shall sing "O my soul, thou hast trodden down strength," we must make fortitude a settled habit, as another of Buchan's noble stories puts it. Nothing less will take us far enough. If "the devastating vice of self-pity" come toward us, walking delicately like Agag, we must hew him in pieces. We shall never know fortitude unless we hate the fondling sin, most devastating of the sins of Christians because most easily disguised under a different name. Few fathom his treacheiies. There can be no compromise with him:

Arise, I say,
Let him come delicately as he may,
Regard him not; but slay.
Away with him.

4

There was a time in the story of Dohnavur when the work which meant far more than life to us all was tossed about and beaten upon like the little ship on the sea of Galilee. It seemed impossible that it should survive, it was so helpless, so defenseless in the eyes of men. One day, it was a very turbulent day, the thought of that ship in the teeth of the gale was like light breaking through the rack that was tearing across the sky, and our hearts kept on saying over and over, "What matter beating wind and tossing billow if only we are in the boat with Thee?" till at last the word was spoken, "Peace, be still"; and there was a great calm.

And so, as one who has known the blowing of the winds, I say to the fearful, "Fear not. There is nothing to fear, nor ever can be, if our Lord be in the boat. O taste and see that the Lord is good: blessed is the man that trusteth in Him. There is nothing too kind for Him to do for the man that trusteth in Him."

The trial of the hour may be of the body, of the mind and spirit, or of circumstances; whatever it be, the same love can comfort: "If your Lord call you to suffering, be not dismayed; there shall be a new allowance of the King for you when you come to it."

We are not at the mercy of wind and wave. We live a double life. Forces of distress may assail us (as they continually assailed our Lord), and we are called to labor from the rising of the morning till the stars appear, and yet all the time in the inner life of the spirit we are marvelously quickened, and raised up and made to sit together in heavenly places in Christ Jesus.

The words *In heavenly places in Christ Jesus* are hung over the door of the room where this book is being written. The room has known many uses. Sick children have been nursed here. It has been office and playroom and prayer room at different hours of the same day. It is no cloistered cell. The words over the door have often helped its owner to live that double life.

5

And so once more we stay our hearts upon our Refuge and Strength, who is our very present help in trouble. Therefore, most blessed *therefore*, we will not fear; for there are always two pines on the hillside of life. One day the last wind will blow. Wind can blow dust in the eyes, but that dust will not blind us: "Yet in my flesh shall I see God: whom I shall see for myself and mine eyes shall behold and not another, not a stranger."

What will it be to see Him whom I have known so long but never seen before? To adore His beauty, to worship Him in holiness; to see Him crowned with glory and honor who was wounded, bruised, oppressed, afflicted, who showed them His hands and His side and said unto them, "Behold My hands and My feet, that it is I Myself"—what will it be to see Him and not another, not a stranger?

What will it be to serve in perfect purity and in untiring vigor? to see no more through a glass darkly, to grope no more on the edge of knowledge, but to press on into that kingdom to which no frontier is set? to see with new eyes, to hear with new ears, to know no more in part but even as also we are known?

What will it be when Faith and Hope fade out of sight and only Love is left? What will it be? We cannot tell. We do not know. Only this we know: the travail of the journey is not worthy to be compared with the glory that shall be revealed to usward, even to usward, though we be the least of the redeemed.

It is the Blessed One and no other who stands by us on the hill when the storm descends upon us. (O Christ, hadst Thou not suffered, how couldst Thou help us now?) And He who suffered and who overcame will grant to us also to overcome. I can think of no truer picture of what we want to be when the wind beats on us for the last time, than this pine, broken and battered, but not uprooted, standing steadfast, undefeated—and not alone.

And now, O my soul, settle it with thyself that thou wilt listen to no hard reports which the ills of this present time may make to thee concerning thy Lord, for "Nothing can come wrong from my Lord in His sweet working." Not clouds and dark woods, for they are lighted; not the deep ravine, for it leads to the heights; not snow, for it can be cherished; not ruin, for "He can make one web of contraries"; not rough waters, for they cannot overflow me; not steep mountains, for when I said, "My foot slippeth," Thy mercy, O Lord, held me up; not dark woods again, for I do not build my nest in any tree on earth; not walls, for they have windows; not storms, for they cannot uproot me; not loneliness, for I am not alone. "Only be thou strong and very courageous": this is Thy word to me, O Lord. "As I was with Moses, so I will be with thee: I will not fail thee nor forsake thee. Be strong and of a good courage." Courage that dares, fortitude that endures—without these I am a reed shaken with the wind. Surely fortitude is the sovereign virtue of life; not patience, though we need it too, but fortitude. O God, give me fortitude.

●   ●   ●

With this my message ends. The next page is only an after-word for the traveler, perhaps quite a young traveler, who has reached the place where the blackbird is singing:

> The blackbird sings to him, "Brother, brother,
>> If this be the last song you shall sing,
> Sing well, for you may not sing another.
>> Brother, sing."

Perhaps for an older one, for whom someone has written this song of faith:

> Gone, they tell me, is youth,
> Gone is the strength of my life.
> Nothing remains but decline,
> Nothing but age and decay.
> Not so, I'm God's little child,
> Only beginning to live;
> Coming the days of my prime,
> Coming the strength of my life,

Coming the vision of God,
Coming my bloom and my power.

Our hope is that these eyes shall see our Lord return: "This same Jesus which is taken up from you into heaven shall so come in like manner as ye have seen Him go into heaven." This is the hope of hopes, but if it be deferred, then "by Thy holy patience we go to Thee who art our crown."

In a certain quiet resting-place in Cumberland there is a small grey stone on which is engraved a question and an answer that seem to me perfect in fitness:

Master, where dwellest Thou?
He saith, Come and see.

The picture of the light in the sky and on the water and the words that belong to it are for the happy traveler who may hope soon to "see."

21

The Last Mile

AND now, Lord, what wait I for? My hope is in Thee. The shadows of the evening are stretched out. The clouds are heavy on the mountains. Thou touchest the hills and they smoke. But like all the clouds of all my life, these heavy clouds are edged with light; and when I look up to the highest cloud I see there no darkness at all, but light, and light beyond light shining down on the peaceful water.

And the water—for I have said to Thee, "Bid me come unto Thee on the water," and Thou hast said, "Come"—that water is a pathway of light. I see a narrow break in the brightness because of the cloud overhead, but soon it is bright again, and then there is no more shadow. And far, far, all but lost in light, I see what I think are other hills, the hills of a better country, even an heavenly.

•   •   •

One evening, as we sat at the end of India on the rocks of Cape Comorin, a little fishing boat sailed into the sunset. It was only a rough thing made of three logs tied together, and its sail was a mere rag, but it was transfigured. To see it so was like seeing the mortal put on immortality, the temporal take on the beauty of the eternal.

Usually, I think, a speck of earth entangled in such glory would show dark against the glory, but that evening, so mighty were the powers of the golden air that all of earth was swallowed up. It was a figure of the true. It held us speechless. As I think of it I hear again the lapping of the waves that filled the silence and see the lighted waters in the afterglow.

But what we call sunset the heavenly people call sunrise, and the Joy of the Lord, and the Morning of God.

Endnotes

1. Deuteronomy 1:31, LXX

2. The Tree of Love, Ramon Lull, translated by E. Allison Peers.

3. So the A.S.V. margin, the German of Luther, and Kay.

4. Jeremiah 38:12.

5. *Lady Victoria Buxton*, a memoir, by G.E.W. Russell.

6. See Westcott on John 14:2.

7. Titus 2:11-12, Arthur Way.

8. Actually, the name was given by the French explorer Jacques Cartier. He took it from the Iroquois word kanata, meaning "a collection of wigwams."

9. Psalm 42:8. Following the A.S.V., the German of Schlachter and the French, which concur in giving this as the meaning: At night a song concerning Him is with me, prayer to the God of my life. The song is the prayer: the prayer is the song.

10. Joshua 23:14, paraphrased.

11. Isaiah 58:12, Rotherham.

12. "It absorbs part of the spectrum of light that passes through it, allowing a greenish light to filter through. It is yellow when viewed by reflected light, as we know. It is very curious that when it has been heated to a dull red heat it becomes permanently transparent, and white by reflected light."—Concerning the Nature of Things, Sir William Bragg.

13. Acts 23:6-10.

14. Psalm 119:65, LXX.

15. Philippians 4:18, 2:25-30.

16. Luke 14:33, Weymouth, 1908 edition.

17. *Oliver Cromwell*, John Buchan.

18. Job 28:25-27, Delitzsch.

Index of First Lines

(Dohnavur songs)

Index

READ THE REMARKABLE STORY OF
the founding of
CLC INTERNATIONAL

Leap of Faith

"Any who doubt that Elijah's God still lives ought to read of the money supplied when needed, the stores and houses provided, and the appearance of personnel in answer to prayer." —Moody Monthly

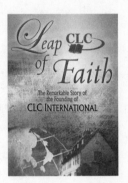

Is it possible that the printing press, the editor's desk, the Christian bookstore and the mail order department can glow with the fast-moving drama of an "Acts of the Apostles"?

Find the answer as you are carried from two people in an upstairs bookroom to a worldwide chain of Christian bookcenters multiplied by nothing but a "shoestring" of faith and by committed, though unlikely, lives.

To order your copy of *Leap of Faith*

You may order by:
Phone: 1-215-542-1240
E-mail: orders@clcpublications.com
Mail: PO Box 1449
Fort Washington, PA 19034

Discount Code: LoF 650
Reg. Price: $11.99
Special Mission Price: $5.40
Shipping in US: $4.00
You pay: $9.40

This book was produced by CLC Publications. We hope it has been life-changing and has given you a fresh experience of God through the work of the Holy Spirit. CLC Publications is an outreach of CLC Ministries International, a global literature mission with work in over fifty countries. If you would like to know more about us or are interested in opportunities to serve with a faith mission, we invite you to contact us at:

CLC Ministries International
PO Box 1449
Fort Washington, PA 19034

_____

Phone: 215-542-1242
E-mail: orders@clcpublications.com
Website: www.clcpublications.com

_ _ _ _ _ _ _ _ _ _ _ _ _ _ _ _ _ _ _ _

DO YOU LOVE GOOD CHRISTIAN BOOKS?
Do you have a heart for worldwide missions?

You can receive a FREE subscription to
CLC's newsletter on global literature missions
Order by e-mail at:

clcworld@clcusa.org

or your request to:

**PO Box 1449
Fort Washington, PA 19034**